The Mystical Experiences of True Buddha Disciples

Master Sheng-yen Lu

Translated by
Siong Ho

Revised and edited by
Janny Chow and K.C. Ng

Amitabha Enterprise, Inc.

San Bruno, California, U.S.A.

i

The Mystical Experiences of True Buddha Disciples

First Edition

© 1993 by Amitabha Enterprise, Inc., San Bruno, California.

Library of Congress Cataloging-in-Publication Data

Lu, Sheng-yen, 1945-
   [Kuei i che ti kan ying. English]
   The Mystical Experiences of True Buddha Disciples / Sheng-yen Lu;
translated by Siong Ho ; revised and edited by Janny Chow and K.C.
Ng. — 1st ed.
      p.   cm.
   Translation of: Kuei i che ti kan ying.
   ISBN 1-881493-01-6 : $ 10.00
   1. Religious life — Chen-fu (Sect) 2. Chen-fu (Sect)   I. Ho,
Siong, 1952- . II. Chow, Janny, 1952- . III. Ng, K.C. (Kwok
C.), 1957- . IV. Title.
   BQ9800.C4892L824413   1993
   294.3'4422 — dc20   93-3807
                                                    CIP

Printed in the United States of America. 1993

A Word From The Master

We know that *physical energy* is a form of external phenomenon and that *mental energy* is an invisible phenomenon. For example, brain waves, thoughts, etc., are invisible energies. If we human beings are able to concentrate and direct our brain waves into physical matter, actually altering the matter, then this is the *inner world* manipulating the *outer world*.

Based on religious practice, during Zen meditation, Holy Red Crown Vajra Master, the Tantric Practitioner, uses visualization, **mudra*** and **mantra** to activate man's primordial potential energy. This activation enables such energy to unite with cosmic energy, producing the great cosmic energy in man.

Religious practice is not *superstition*; rather, it is a scientific practice of *inner illumination*. The practice of Zen meditation is, indeed, a great science among the sciences.

---

* Terms defined in the Glossary are printed in boldface where they first appear in the text.

Contents

Contents (Cont.)

Acknowledgements

The Amitabha Enterprise, Inc. would like to thank the following for making this translation possible:

Grand Master Sheng-yen Lu (Living Buddha Lian-shen) for His blessing and guidance; Master Lian-tze, Master Lian-han, and Master Samantha Chou for their encouragement; Siong Ho for all his hard work in the original translation; Janny Chow and Kwok C. Ng for revising the translated manuscript; Pamela Ziv Johnson for editing and technical advice; Tannie Liu and Kevin Henderson for their valuable advice; Cecilia Chung, Lawrence Chong, Hector Campbell, and Grace Yang for their involvement in bringing this project to its present book form.

The Mystical Experiences of True Buddha Disciples

Preface — A True Personal Statement

The Holy Red Crown Vajra Master Sheng-yen Lu, the Tantric Practitioner, currently has 70,000 students[1] around the world. Undoubtedly, in the future, this number will greatly multiply to tens of millions.

There is a profound affinity between **Amitabha Buddha** and Master Sheng-yen Lu. Due to the great vow and compassion of White **Padmakumara**, the **Dharma Body** of Master Sheng-yen Lu, Amitabha Buddha has especially asked White Padmakumara of the **Maha** Twin Lotus Ponds to descend to the human world to turn the great Dharma Wheel of salvation. It is hoped that sentient beings, upon seeing and hearing the profound Buddha Dharma, will gradually know and practice it, thus enabling themselves to be salvaged by Amitabha's Pure Land.

The Amitabha Sutra says:

"If a virtuous man or woman hears of *Amitabha* and persistently upholds his name, whether for one day, two days, three days, four days, five days, six days, or seven days and, if the mind is unified and not disconcerted, then, when such a person is dying, Amitabha and his retinue will appear before him. When such a person dies, if his mind is free of contrary thoughts, he will be reborn in Amitabha's Paradise of Ultimate Bliss [Sukhavati]."

This part of the sutra is genuine, the merits to be

---

[1] As of 1993, there are over 1,000,000 students all around the world who have taken refuge in Grand Master Lu.

1

derived from it are inconceivable, and all Buddhas are mindful of them. The Maha Twin Lotus Ponds are among the most magnificent scenes of the Western Paradise of Ultimate Bliss. Padmakumara (Lotus Child) is the Lotus **Bodhisattva**. It is similar if one hears the name of Padmakumara and desires to be born in the Maha Twin Lotus Ponds. If one can just uphold the Padmakumara's Heart Mantra and practice the Padmakumara Yoga and, if one's mind is calm and free from contrary thoughts, then one will be reborn in the Pure Land of the Maha Twin Lotus Ponds.

It is true that all Buddhas are mindful of this. The merits are inconceivable and rare. It is the most remarkable way of salvation in today's world. The Dharma of the True Buddha School is the same as that of Amitabha, sharing the same goals, interests and merits.

The founder of the True Buddha School, the Holy Red Crown Vajra Master, is a teacher of right belief in Buddha Dharma. He instructs people to approach the auspicious and avoid the disastrous, to perform good deeds, and to achieve the **Six Transcendental Powers**. He teaches people to understand the **karmic** law (law of Cause and Effect) of the past, present, and future, to lead directly to man's true-self, to salvage and liberate all sentient beings from suffering in the cycles of birth and death, so that everyone can ascend to the Maha Twin Lotus Ponds of the Buddha kingdom.

Due to his great vow and compassion, **Vajra** Master Lian-shen (the refuge name of Master Sheng-yen Lu) is protected and assisted by all Buddhas. His work of salvation is manifested in immeasurable and inexhaustible ways. Incidents are frequently noted where disciples have received psychic responses from Master Lian-shen. Word of the wonderful manifestations of Padmakumara and of the countless mystical experiences have caused uproars

2

everywhere.

The manifestations of Vajra Master Sheng-yen Lu, the **Transformation Body** of Padmakumara, are wondrous happenings. Students who have experienced these, themselves, through sight or sound, all know these manifestations to be real. The impossible has become possible, and inconceivable miracles have occurred.

Because there is a large number of mystical experiences which are happening to the initiated, I only selected those in which the mystical experience was strong and the experience verifiable. I noted these manifestations page by page to ensure that readers would know that the Buddha Dharma of the True Buddha School and the psychic responses from the Holy Red Crown Vajra Master are genuine.

I have often remarked that one kind of rice can feed one hundred kinds of people. There are many miracles and many sincere disciples. However, some obstinate skeptics of Buddhism still do not believe this. I hope such readers will abandon this prejudiced view and read this book objectively, humbly seeking verification. If you realize verification, your doubts will be cleared from you and you will certainly want to take refuge in the Holy Red Crown Vajra Master and the True Buddha School. You will become one of the devotees, find Truth, and experience the mystical experience.

All students of the True Buddha School are of the lineage of Master Lian-shen, who has attained Realization. The White Padmakumara of the Maha Twin Lotus Ponds is [an emanation of] the Dharma body of Master Lian-shen. To receive mystical experience, one must sincerely believe this.

If an initiated student, (following the great vow of Master Lian-shen and his spirit of salvaging the world), makes, with compassion and loving kindness, a great vow to liberate sentient beings, he should first commit no evil deeds, and then perform all virtuous deeds. That is, one should eliminate one's *greed, anger* and *ignorance*, and then practice the **Six Perfections** (**Paramitas**) of the Bodhisattvas. In Dharma practice (**sadhana**), one starts with the Four Preliminaries, continues with the Guru Yoga, then the Personal Deity Yoga, and finally achieves response in the great Vajra Yoga and the Highest Yoga **Tantra**.

Practice daily and consistently, as consistently as one takes ones meals, because Dharma practice is nutrition for the mind. Strive to progress. One will receive the light from the Buddhas and Bodhisattvas, purifying one's negative **karma** and eliminating misfortunes, while increasing one's blessings and wisdom.

Eventually, the wonderful psychic responses from the Holy Red Crown Vajra Master Lian-shen will manifest themselves, and miracles will occur. One who experiences these will gain more confidence. Any student of the True Buddha School who has psychic responses should treat them as an encouragement, not become attached to them by becoming complacent. Further, students should humbly improve themselves, pursuing the correct results, and attaining Supreme Perfect Enlightenment.

The mystical experiences of refuge students which are contained in this book are completely factual. However, due to fear for their reputations, some students do not wish their names to be published. Therefore, some fictitious names have been used instead of real ones. This is unavoidable and I hope readers will understand.

To help a confused world we need real occurrences of mystical experiences. Today there exist not only despicable minds, murders, robberies, and sexual assaults, but also heavy emphasis is placed by people on personal fame and gain. Where many disasters occur, theories alone are

4

not sufficient. Some Dharma preachers depend on theories alone, expounding only on them, but listeners will not believe them because there are no facts to support the theories. Some people condemn mystical experiences as manifestations of evil spirits. As a matter of fact, mystical experiences are phenomena which are part of Buddha Dharma practices. Many practitioners only start to believe and practice sincerely after they have had mystical experiences.

Mystical experience is an expedient means for the Bodhisattvas to help all beings release themselves from sufferings. This view has been misunderstood by many "left-home people" (monks), who are unable to receive mystical experiences themselves, and so condemn them as evil occurrences. True Buddha practitioners should strive to *awaken to their original nature* and *transcend life and death*. It is only through actual practice that one receives mystical experience, perfect understanding, enlightenment, and the attainment of the supreme Buddha path.

Those of you who, having obtained and read my spiritual books, honestly believe Venerable Master Lian-shen to be an enlightened person, believe the True Buddha School to be a true Buddhist sect, and would like to have a master for life-time guidance, please take refuge according to the refuge procedure. Send your name, address and age to the following permanent mailing address (with an offering of any amount). You will then receive the actual lineage of the True Buddha School.

Sheng-yen Lu
17102 NE 40th Ct.
Redmond, WA 98052
U.S.A.

Redmond, Washington, U.S.A.
May 1985

1. My First Travel Through The Illusory Realm of the Great Void

In April, 1975, I published my first spiritual book entitled *Experiences in Spiritual Reading.* One of the chapters in that book is called "Traveling through the Illusory Realm[1] of the Great Void."

This was my first experience in traveling through the Illusory Realm of the Great Void. I was only twenty-five years old, more than ten years ago now. To quote from the text of that experience:

"So much had happened that day that I went to bed thinking about it all. I couldn't fall asleep right away. Suddenly, I smelled the fragrance of sandalwood. I closed my eyes. In a trance, I saw a circle of light as bright as a mirror, surrounded by a shimmering golden aura. At that moment, my body seemed to float in the air and through the circle of light. I could only hear the wind blowing and it began to feel as if I had flown a very long distance. Suddenly I realized I was in *a different dimension.* Indeed, I had entered a world of a different dimension.

"Somehow it was clear to me, that this was the Illusory Realm of the Great Void, and that I was touring the Illusory Realm under the guidance of a certain force. I met many Bodhisattvas whom I could not recognize. They bowed in salutation. I saw lotus flowers as large

---

[1] Illusory Realm here refers to a realm that is manifested out of the Void.

as car wheels, in many colors, and on every lotus flower stood a child. Each child held in its hand a lotus of a different color. Ladders, surrounded by gods clad in gold armor, came down from the space above. A beautiful mist floated up from the ground. I saw elaborately carved abodes adorned with gold, silver and crystal — their resplendent lights cascading all over the ground. I saw two pillars that stretched up to the clouds. A voice spoke in my ear saying that one pillar represented K'unlun Mountain and the other represented the Sumeru[2]."

As I stated previously this is part of the chapter "Traveling through the Illusory Realm of the Great Void," from my book *Experiences in Spiritual Reading*. It was written more then ten years ago, about an experience that occurred when I was twenty-five years old. At that time, I was a young man. Now, I am middle-aged. The reason I again bring up this occurrence is to offer it as evidence. The following sentences are the account of Padmakumara. "I saw lotus flowers as large as car wheels, in many colors, and on every lotus flower stood a child. Each child held in its hand a different colored lotus." In that chapter, I have disclosed my previous life.

Was traveling through the Illusory Realm of the Great Void real? At the time I told only two people what had happened. They were my parents. I remember my father said, "Born from a lotus, born from a lotus, isn't it the Third Prince Nata?[3]" My father had read stories about Chinese gods and thought that a child born from

---

[2] According to Taoist cosmology, whoever ascends the K'unlun Mountain reaches the heavens. In Buddhist cosmology, Sumeru is a mountain at the center of the universe. The two pillars seen side by side here thus represent an integration of Taoist and Buddhist philosophy in Master Lu's upcoming spiritual growth.

[3] The Third Prince Nata is a figure in Chinese mythology.

a lotus must be the Third Prince Nata.

In the intervening ten years I have changed from a young man to a middle-aged man, and I have cultivated to the stage of the Holy Red Crown Vajra Master, Lianshen the Tantric Practitioner. Still, these events seem as if they just happened yesterday. Some people think that Sheng-yen Lu is someone who only talks about ghosts and deities, thus his words are not true. But I say, "My vow is to liberate sentient beings even if I will be smashed[4] into pieces! My traveling through the Illusory Realm of the Great Void, my awareness of my previous lives and of the incarnation of Padmakumara (because of his vow) are all true."

If someone were to threaten my life with a gun or a knife, to force me to say that those events are false, I would choose death rather than lie. This is because what I saw was real, clear, vivid and comprehensible. All Buddhas and Bodhisattvas are my witnesses!

I want to tell the reader that I and my holy title are, indeed, genuine and unique:

The Western Lotus Ponds Assembly[5], the Maha

---

[4] Here Master Lu is talking about his vow to teach Tantric Buddhism. Although Tantric Buddhism has long been known to lead a person to Buddhahood in this life, it has been well guarded and cloaked in complete secrecy. Traditionally, the secrets are only revealed to people who are spiritually ready; now Master Lu is willing to teach the essence of Tantra to anyone who is willing to learn. Thus he is willing to accept any retribution that may be caused by his deviation from traditions, even if he is to be pulverized into small particles.

[5] This refers to the assembly of Buddhas and Bodhisattvas in the Western Paradise of Amitabha, Sukhavati. Within Amitabha Buddha's Western Paradise exist two very large lotus ponds and within those ponds there are eighteen great Padmakumaras, including one robed in white, i.e. Master Lu.

Twin Lotus Ponds, the Eighteen Maha Padmaku-
maras, the Holy Revered One Robed in White, the
Holy Red Crown Vajra Master, the Secret Ruler of
the Realm of Mantra, the Great Enlightened Founder
of Ling Shen True Buddha School, the Illustrious
***Tantrika** Sheng-yen Lu.*

My Dharma Body (Self Nature Body), permanent
and indestructible, is in the Maha Twin Lotus Ponds.
My Bliss Body, which has already attained inner Dharma
happiness, fills the whole universe and is able to respond
to needs. My Transformation Body is an emanation of
Padmakumara who, according to the needs of the sentient
beings, appears in the world to liberate all beings.

Why do people still disbelieve? The True Buddha
School is such a great Dharma cause, with so many genuine cases of mystical experiences. Why do people still
refuse to believe? The Buddha Dharma is boundless and
is for helping all humanity, but only *belief* can lead people
to it. Those who take refuge in Holy Red Crown Vajra
Master are those who believe in the existence of the Padmakumara. Their Tantric cultivation will not fail and,
in having the right belief, they also obtain mystical experiences. The opening of this Dharma gate leads to the
unexcelled Truth of the great Buddhist path. Let us all
chant together, *"Om ah hum, guru bei, ah ho sa sa maha,
Lian-shen siddhi hum."*

Perhaps some people might wonder which Bodhisattva is Padmakumara. In fact, Padmakumara is
a transformation of "the Pure Eye **Tathagata.**" The
samadhi of this Buddha is based on the Universal Eye
of Great Compassion, observing and responding to all
sentient beings, guiding them to become Buddhas themselves. The light of his compassionate eye shines everywhere. Its Tantric title is Buddha Victory Vajra. In

Tantric Buddhism, it is "The All Buddha Eye of the Great Vajra that constitutes the Auspicious Mother of all Buddhas," that is, the Venerable Buddha Locana. Her merits are truly great. It is the "Great Diamond of the Auspicious Mother of all Buddhas," which is "Buddha-eye Sage." Her merits, too, are truly great.[6]

The Venerable Buddha Locana is transformed into the Eighteen Padmakumaras, and the transformation bodies of the Eighteen Padmakumaras have appeared in the world to help sentient beings — this is the remarkable Dharma Cause. The great salvation Dharma being proclaimed by Vajra Master Sheng-yen Lu is more than an ordinary act of faith, it requires Guru-devotion, Treasuring the Dharma, and Actual Practice. This is an extraordinary opportunity for a true, universal salvation.

The Universal Eye of Great Compassion is like a great sun radiating light and energy. The great power of Padmakumara is unimaginable, and similar to that of every Bodhisattva. He brings peace and comfort to the bodies and minds of all beings.

In order to assist and prove the existence of Amitabha of the Western Paradise of Ultimate Bliss, Padmakumara has incarnated in the human realm to spread these teachings. He has all the wisdom of the Tathagata to cleanse negative karmas and end worries. It is a powerful wisdom that will accomplish great things.

Padmakumara holds a preaching mudra in his right hand, which is to teach and save all beings. His left hand holds a lotus mudra which is the attainment of

---

[6] This paragraph contains various titles of Buddha Locana. Buddha Locana is Sanskrit for Buddha Eye, and she is an expression of the Great Sun Buddha — Vairocana. It is through the eyes that pure awareness in the heart is expressed and perceived as radiance or streams of light.

the fruit of Padmakumara. The great Dharma cause of Padmakumara to save all sentient beings is pouring the great Dharma rain, blowing the great Dharma conch, beating the great Dharma drum, and displaying the great Dharma meanings. Padmakumara is the Lotus Child and also the venerable Buddha Locana, who is also the Worthy of Worship, the Omniscient, the Knowledge-Conduct-Perfect, the Well-Gone, the Knower of the Worlds, the Peerless One, the Master of Taming, the Teacher of **devas** and men, and Buddha.

The Buddha power of Padmakumara fills boundless and immeasurable time and space. Padmakumara has emitted his Light to prompt all beings to take refuge and be saved; therefore, I, Master Sheng-yen Lu, will write spiritual books — one after another.

Here is a verse:

> *Traveling leisurely through the Great Void,*
> *The Buddha eyes of Padmakumara*
> *See the destiny of this remarkable Dharma*
> *cause,*
> *To save heavenly and worldly beings and those*
> *in the Nether worlds.*

This is the great salvation of both heaven and earth.

2. A Whole Monastery Takes Refuge

This should be an ordinary story but, from the ordinary, a trace of the extraordinary is revealed....

It happened in a rural monastery in Southern Taiwan. The monastery is located half-way up a mountain. With many, huge apple trees surrounding it, the setting provides an ideal atmosphere for spiritual practices.

A young lady from a wealthy family was staying in the monastery. In the quiet atmosphere she prayed to the Buddhas and studied in preparation for the university entrance examination. In addition to the textbooks she had to study, she had also brought along some religious literature, including a few of my spiritual books.

At this time some strange events began to happen.

One night, the abbot of the monastery dreamed that he was walking around inside the monastery. He came to the door of this wealthy young lady and saw her reading a book which was not a textbook nor a Buddhist scripture. Strangest of all, this book emitted billions of rays of golden light, which were so strong that he had to close his eyes. He woke up as a result of this.

Although the abbot felt the dream was strange, he did not concern himself about it. The following night, however, he had the same dream again. This he did not understand and he began to wonder. The third night he had the same dream again. He decided to investigate, believing that the dream must contain some unusual meaning. What a person dreams once cannot be considered

12

unusual. For the same dream to occur twice is a little strange. When it occurs three times, one must look into it.

Restless, the abbot went to the young lady's quiet, secluded room and saw her reading a book. Her back was to him. He thought that this was just like what he had seen in the dream. Then, the young lady saw the abbot. She rose immediately and bowed to him.

"What book are you reading?" He asked.

"It's...it's..." she replied, hiding the gold-lettered, chocolate-colored book behind her. She hesitated, feeling uneasy.

"Let me see the book; I will tell no one," the abbot said.

The young lady handed the book to him. When he looked at it, he saw it was a book written by Master Sheng-yen Lu, entitled *The Method of **Vajrayana**.*

"Do you know Sheng-yen Lu?" The abbot asked.

She said, "I have not met him, but I find his writings make a lot of sense. I wrote to him to request refuge and I have received remote-empowerment from him. I am practicing the Guru Yoga, reciting the Guru Heart Mantra and reading his books to learn the Dharma."

"Before I became a monk, I heard many things about him, mostly criticisms, from many great monks. They said Sheng-yen Lu had gone astray and become possessed by demons, but I have not yet read his books. Since you have his books here, which is really wonderful, would you lend me some to read?"

She was extremely happy to hear this. From her luggage she removed *The Realization of the Master, The **Bon** Religion and Sorcery, Highest Yoga Tantra* and ***Mahamudra**, A Little Taste of Zen, Between Buddha and **Mara***, and others, and handed them to the abbot.

Once the abbot started to read them, he found, to

13

his surprise, that he was reluctant to put them down. He read them day and night, whenever he had time. He was totally absorbed in reading them, like someone who had found the Truth.

The abbot told the young lady that the teaching of Buddha was inconceivable and the power of Master Lu was unimaginable. Master Lu's books were written in simple words. Every sentence was clear and comprehensible. They were not books written by someone who had gone astray and become possessed by demons. Master Lu had great compassion. He was not a liar and not an evil person, as had been rumored outside.

The abbot ordered all nine monks and nuns in the monastery to set up an incense table in the monastery's main hall. For the next three days, they burned incense, while praying and chanting the Great Compassion Dharani one hundred eight times. Feeling everything empty, and free from the grasp of prejudices, the abbot sincerely knelt down with all the monks and nuns, asking permission from the Thousand-armed and Thousand-eyed **Avalokitesvara (Kuan Yin)** Bodhisattva to allow them to take refuge in Master Sheng-yen Lu of Redmond, Washington, USA, who was the incarnation of Padmakumara.

Then, they used the prophecy blocks, a method of divination, and received seven holy blocks, which meant the Thousand-armed and Thousand-eyed Avalokitesvara Bodhisattva had granted approval.

Then, a stranger thing happened. On the night of the approval by the Thousand-armed and Thousand-eyed Avalokitesvara Bodhisattva, all nine monks and nuns saw, in their dreams, the Holy Red Crown Vajra Master sitting magnificently on a lotus, amid auspicious clouds. Wearing a Five-Buddha-Crown, the Master emitted a billion rays of golden light and was surrounded by many Dakinis (sky-dancers) who waited upon him.

Interestingly, one of the nuns had a growth on her neck, which had been hard and visible to everyone. After the dream about Master Lu, the growth became soft, shrunken, and gradually began to disappear. The abbot mailed a list to me in America of all the names of the monks and nuns. He requested initiations and remote empowerment and detailed his reasons for doing so.

This is an absolutely true story.

In the past, there have been many people who have taken refuge due to dreams, and some of these have been mentioned in my previous spiritual books. One such person is General Wang Lien of Taipei, author of *Maintain the Health by Taoist Breathing Exercises*, *Curing through Taoist Breathing Exercises*, and other books. In Toronto, Canada, there was Chao Li Ch'an, and in Edmonton, Canada, there was Liang Yung Ming and other lay Buddhists. People who have taken refuge through dreams had the ritual of refuge done first in the dreams, then later they came to seek refuge in person.

There are many more monks and nuns who have taken refuge through remote empowerment. For example, recently there was Dharma Master Shakya Kuo Hsien, the abbot of Hui Ch'uan monastery in Hong Kong, Dharma Master Nai Tung of P'u Men Pao En Monastery in Thailand, Shakya Wu Chin and Shakya Hui P'o (mentioned in my previous spiritual books). In fact, there were many more from all over the world. Some of these monks and nuns did not want their initiation publicized. I understand their circumstances and therefore do not reveal their names in my books.

When monks and nuns took refuge in me and asked for advice, my replies were sent in plain, white envelopes, without my name and address on them, so that the students would be spared sarcastic remarks from other monks and nuns. Sometimes my replies had to be sent via a third party instead of directly to the monastery. This was to avoid unnecessary troubles, as it was not easy for many of the monks and nuns to seek refuge in me.

It was a rare occurrence for a whole monastery of monks and nuns to come to take refuge. This was a destiny that was a direct result of my book, *The Method of Vajrayana,* which emitted golden ray in the dreams of the abbot.

The seven holy blocks approval of the Thousand-armed and Thousand-eyed Avalokitesvara Bodhisattva, the dream about the Master by the nine monks and nuns, and the disappearance of the nun's neck growth — these are all great mystical experiences.

I would like to disclose the name of this monastery and of its abbot; however, the abbot requested in his letter to me that I withhold their names from the public, as the high monk who ordained the abbot into monkhood still harbors misunderstandings toward me. I understand the abbot's difficulties and I beg the reader's forgiveness for keeping the names secret.

3. The Advance Notice of the Fire Deva

If residents of Tai-chung have not forgotten, they should recall a moderate fire that broke out on Nanking Road that had started in the building of the First Credit Co-operative Association. The fire spread to the right, burning four or five stores in succession, and ended at the International Electrical Appliances store.

It was daytime when the buildings caught fire. At that time, I was still living in Taiwan.

Approximately two years before the fire, I was at the International Electrical Appliances store to check the **Feng Shui** of the area. It was the owner, not the tenant, of the store who had invited me to conduct a Feng Shui investigation. The owner was a woman whose husband had died some years previously.

I remember that she took me to the second floor, where there was an altar for gods, and I joined my palms before the altar. Unexpectedly, a strange thing happened. I saw the Fire Deva, who is one of the deities called upon in Tantric fire offerings. Its Sanskrit name is "Agni," and he is one of the Eight Devas at the eight points of the compass. The Fire Deva was riding a black oxen, his whole body was red in color, with flames surrounding him. He had four arms, one holding a green bamboo, one a water jug, one was held with the palm up, and one held the **mala**. I saw his body flames spread out and turn into natural fire, burning up the entire building.

I was astonished and told the owner, "This house is

going to be destroyed by fire."

"When?" Her face tuned pale.

"Two years from now," I said assuredly.

I felt bad after telling her and I knew she also felt very bad. It was a slip of the tongue — I spoke without a second thought because I actually saw both the Fire Deva and the destruction of the building in a huge fire. The smoke was dense, the fire was fierce, the pillars burned one after another, and the whole building collapsed.

There was a time when I pondered whether it was right for me to make prophecies, especially ones like this. To tell people that their houses were going to burn down was frightening to those who had invited me to conduct Feng Shui.

After the owner heard what I said, her face turned pale and blank. I knew she was sad and I regretted making the prophecy in such a direct manner.

After my prophecy of the Fire Deva, the owner leased out the store to the International Electrical Appliances and moved herself to another location. She did so mainly because of the prophecy I made.

However, this woman did not come to see me for the next two years, probably because she did not know whether she should believe me or not. Probably she did not trust me.

From what I heard later, the fire at Nanking Road was caused by sparks in electrical wires. The fire broke out at the First Credit Co-operative Association and spread towards the right and finally destroyed the International Electrical Appliances store.

Two years after my prophecy, the owner came back to me.

"It was all burned down, right?" I said.

"Luckily, I moved all the furniture out," she said. "How come your prediction was so accurate?"

"I saw the Fire Deva," I said. "Why are you here again?"

"I want to sell the burnt down lot as soon as possible, so I especially came to seek your help," she replied.

Who can ever prove this incident? This woman is the best witness. In addition, Mr. Hu-ts'ung Chou and his wife, Luan Ch'en, of #31- 301 Alley, Yung He Street in Tai-chung also knew about the prophecy. They are relatives of the owner and are the ones who had suggested that she come to me about Feng Shui. Mr. Hu-ts'ung Chou was the manager of the P'uli Branch of the Medium and Small Business Bank.

As a result of my accurate prediction, they all came to take refuge in the Holy Red Crown Vajra Master. They realized that every act and word of the Master was verifiable. My prediction that the house would burn down in two years was not made casually. I couldn't have known if I had not actually seen the vision.

Incidents of such accurate predictions are innumerable. My miraculous predictions became well-known in Taiwan. While I was still there, about three hundred people came each day to see me. As soon as the door was opened early in the morning, crowds of visitors would stream into my apartment, and I could only give three to five minutes to each individual.

After arriving in the States, my ability of divination also became well known here. People from all over the world came to see me, and my name became known internationally. During this time [in the States], I again saw the Fire Deva descending onto a Westerner's home. Once again I voiced my prediction. They believed me and immediately moved out. Again the prediction was right; their former home burned. The whole family came to take refuge in the Holy Red Crown Vajra Master.

To predict that someone's house will burn down is

definitely not a welcome thing, but, as the proverb says, *It is the unforeseen that always happens.* Unfortunate events do occur. In the eyes of the Master such events are karma, destined to happen.

When help can be given, I try to do my best to help. Furthermore, as *creatures grieve their fellow creatures*, I try my best to help those who come to me. But, it's the karma! Once I see the Fire Deva, I know there will be a visit of fire.

One student asked, "Why can't the Master ask the Fire Deva not to come?"

"In the wisdom eye of the Buddha, karma is unavoidable."

"How would you explain this?"

I replied, "Despite the great spiritual power Master has, and the many miracles that are done to help people, spiritual power is ineffective when it encounters karma. The relationship between cause and effect involved in karma can be extremely complicated. To discuss this in detail would take a considerable amount of time. Karma will definitely happen, and Master can only help transfer it or reduce the damage. In this respect, it very much requires the faith of the parties involved, or taking refuge in Master and learning the unexcelled Tantric Dharma to transfer the karma."

What a wonder! The Holy Red Crown Vajra Master Lian-shen, the Tantric Practitioner, saw the Fire Deva and predicted the fires — facts that can be verified by anyone. Master is the manifestation of Padmakumara and the founder of the True Buddha School. In the future, there will be thousands of masters from the True Buddha School giving help to people. The True Buddha School is an unexcelled, great Dharma Cause for the whole world.

4. An Apparition's Call

Ever since she was initiated, Lian-ching of Chile, South America has been diligently practicing Guru Yoga. She is a school teacher and has also brought several Spanish-speaking people to take refuge in the True Buddha School.

One day, while reading in her own study, she suddenly felt tired. She fell asleep and saw her deceased mother appear before her.

Lian-ching's mother had worked hard all her life but she was not a believer of Buddhism. While alive, she ran a chicken farm and had slaughtered innumerable chickens for sale. Lian-ching vividly saw her mother standing in front of her. Her mother was wearing some very old, tattered clothes, and she looked sad, as if she were sick and poor.

Her mother told Lian-ching that she was receiving punishments in the nether world because she had not believed in anything while she was alive, and because she had killed many lives. Many spirits came after her. Now, without any possessions, she was acutely ill all the time and had to perform hard labor everyday, a consequence of not believing in karma. One day, a spirit guard told her secretly, "Your daughter has taken refuge in the True Buddha School and become a disciple of a real Vajra-master who has great merits. If Lian-ching asked the Vajra master to perform a deliverance for you, you wouldn't have to suffer in here."

Lian-ching's mother lamentedly begged her and, in the dream, Lian-ching herself was embracing her mother.

With tears on her face, and crying this way, she woke up.

Lian-ching is by nature a very filial girl. She couldn't bear to see the way her mother had suffered in the dream and thought of writing to the Master, to beg him to do the deliverance for her mother. But, when she thought about it again, it seemed to be only a dream, and the number of people who sought help from the Vajra-master was so great. Thinking about how busy Master must be, Lian-ching did not want to bother him. After all, it was just a dream. Thinking about her mother and Master, she could not make up her mind, and so it dragged on for a few days.

One day while Lian-ching was still indecisive, her older sister, who lived nearby, came to the door and told her about also having a dream of their mother. In the dream their mother repeated the words, "Shu-yun is disobedient,...Shu-yun is disobedient...." This was repeated continuously. (Shu-yun is Lian-ching's real name.)

Because of this unusual dream, Lian-ching's sister had come to tell her about it. Such a coincidence made Lian-ching decide to write to the Master. She detailed everything in her letter and enclosed a photo of her mother, her mother's birth date, the date she passed away, and location of where she was buried, together with a fee for the offerings in the deliverance ritual.

After receiving her letter, I placed her mother's photo, as well as the best offerings to the Buddhas on the altar. I followed the procedure of deliverance, wrote and burned a Prayer. I sincerely invoked all Buddhas and Bodhisattvas. The gist of that Prayer is as follows:

"To all Buddhas and Bodhisattvas of the Ten Directions and Three Times, all the great holy sages always abiding in the Ten Directions, please, with your holy eyes, I beg you to guide all sentient beings with compassion, and hope that you will not relinquish the vow of compassion. Please descend onto the altar and accept Lian-ching's wonderful offerings. Now there is Lian-ching's mother who is in extreme torture in the nether world. Without any possessions, help, or protection, she is also inflicted with illnesses. All the negative karmas she created in life are appearing to her in the nether world. Involuntarily she is being punished by the spirit guards.

"Lian-ching's mother now being initiated in the True Buddha School as witnessed by its founder, the Holy Red Crown Vajra Master Lian-shen, the Tantric Practitioner, who wishes that all Buddhas and Bodhisattvas would emit immense brightness with compassion to save her mother and to endow her with great empowerments, so as to release her from her extreme suffering in the nether world. Sages of great compassion and mercy, please release her quickly from her sufferings."

(At this moment, Master performed the ritual with the Great Vajra Compassion Hook. With the power of the Great Compassion Hook, her soul was drawn away from her bad karmas. This is like a drowning person being hooked by the clothes and pulled to the shore by a rescuer.)

During the course of this ritual practice, brightness appeared from the nether world. The spirit guards of the nether world clasped their palms and chanted together:

We all bow to the venerable Lian-shen,
Who apparently resides in the human world,
In the form of a Master to salvage all beings
And to liberate those in the nether world.
We all bow to the great venerable Lian-shen,
Who preaches the fine Dharmas with a mighty voice,
Points out the perfect path of nirvana,
And helps all beings to obtain the fruit of enlighten-
   ment.

These spirit guards of the nether world clasped their palms and lauded, "The Western Lotus Ponds Assembly, the Maha Twin Lotus Ponds, the Eighteen Mahapadmakumaras, the Holy Revered One Robed in White, the Holy Red Crown Vajra Master, the Secret Ruler of the Realm of Vajra Mantra, the Enlightened Founder of Ling Shen True Buddha School, the Illustrious Tantrika, Sheng-yen Lu."

Then, from the sky, the World of Ultimate Bliss of Buddha World appeared. Suddenly, a ray of golden light came down and lifted up Lian-ching's mother. Her mother saw a four-armed white Kuan Yin Bodhisattva, smiling, wearing the Five-Buddha Crown on her head, dressed in a celestial gown and necklaces, and looking magnificent. The golden light came from the mala in her hand.

Lian-ching's mother chanted respectfully, "Namo Kuan Shih Yin Bodhisattva, Namo Kuan Shih Yin Bodhisattva, ..."

This deliverance was performed daily for a week, yielding perfect merits.

Lian-ching did not dream of her mother again, neither did her sister. Only once, while Lian-ching was bowing to the White Kuan Yin Bodhisattva in the temple and chanting the mantra of the White Kuan Yin Bodhisattva, she suddenly saw white lights emitting from the top of the head of the Bodhisattva. In front of the White Kuan Yin Bodhisattva, there appeared a lotus with someone sitting cross-legged on it. This person was wearing a gray cloak like Lian-ching's mother used to wear and the person looked very much like her mother. But she disappeared almost immediately.

Lian-ching reasoned that the deliverance ritual performed by the Vajra Master had released her mother from her sufferings. Kuan Yin Bodhisattva had shown her that her mother had already gone riding the lotus. Lian-ching told her sister about this, who also thought it was wonderful. Her sister had taken refuge before in other Tulkus, Lamas, and Vajra masters; now she wanted to take refuge in the True Buddha School. She now believed the Holy Red Crown Vajra Master to be a real master and she was willing to take refuge in another real vajra master.

The spiritual power of deliverance is unlimited in a real vajra master. Real vajra masters are actually the incarnations of Buddhas and Bodhisattvas. They appear in all kinds of manifestations, which are expedient ways of leading all beings from suffering to happiness.

Birth, aging, sickness, and death in the human world and the **Six Realms** of cyclic existence are full of immense suffering. This is because of the effects of the Eight Desires and Angers. For the One Great Cause, the Master has emerged in this world. He is fearless of all slanders and will salvage many beings. Slander only impels him to progress more vigorously because he is a truly Enlightened person. Let us hope everyone will cross the river to the other shore to attain the bodhi, to act according to the Buddha's teachings, and liberate both the living and the deceased.

5. A Happy Lottery Winner

On page 124 of my book, *The Great Spanning Rainbow of Magical Charms*, is a **charm**, the "jackpot winning charm." When the book came out, many students requested it so they could wear the charm. In Taiwan, people buy a "Patriot Prize." Overseas, many students buy lottery or horse racing tickets.

It was not my purpose in printing this charm in *The Great Spanning Rainbow of Magical Charms* to make people greedy or get them involved in gambling. However, among my students, there are some who are confronted with extreme monetary difficulties, and who are at the end of their rope. If they sincerely pray, they might receive Master's empowerment, and luck might come to them.

Have any of the students won a lottery jackpot or a first prize ticket? Yes, there have been winners. Obviously I cannot reveal the names and addresses of the grand prize winners for fear of extortion, robbery or fraudulent charitable organizations, which might generate all sorts of problems. Therefore, grand prize winners will not be named. Students who have won such prizes secretly inform me in writing about their good fortune. They are extremely happy.

In this chapter, I will reveal a medium prize winner from Taipei. This student is Mr. Chih-ch'i Tai. His refuge name is Lian-chan. His address is: #58-3, Alley 11, Ln 188, Sec 1, Wenhua Rd, Pan Ch'iao, Taipei. He won a fourth prize in the Patriot Prize.

His letter to me follows:

Dear Master Lian-shen,

When the company I worked for was liquidated, I lost my job and had no income. I was both sick and poor; however, my situation made me more attentive to my practice of the "Jambhala Yoga" with which you empowered me. There is always a way out. On the day my baby son turned one month old, I bought a Patriot Prize ticket which I placed before the Buddha. After the draw, the ticket turned out to be a fourth prize winner totaling three hundred thousand (Taiwan) dollars, and netting two hundred forty thousand dollars after taxes. Even though I haven't found a job yet, this money can sustain us for some time.

I promised before the Buddha that, if I won a prize, I would put more effort into my practice and make offerings to the Vajra Master to help cover the expenses of Dharma propagation. Meanwhile, I beg Master to bless me and, when my financial situation improves later, I promise to make my offerings again.

A few days ago, I obtained from a Dharma brother a statue of the Jambhala for my altar. Now I have plenty of time to practice, and my confidence has increased greatly. Meanwhile, I hope Master will empower me in the Guru Yoga and the Black Wealth Deity Yoga. I hope Master will give me special blessings so I can find a job soon to make a living properly.

May you be as happy as Buddha.
Sincerely,
Disciple Lian-chan

In this chapter, I especially wish to emphasize a few points:

I hope every one of my students is free from poverty. I do not wish them to face financial predicaments. Sometimes, the impact of unsuccessful careers may affect the confidence of the practitioners. Therefore, poor students should enshrine on their altar the statue of Padmakumara, the Vajra of Great Blessing, or the Four Celestial Kings, or the Yellow, Red, White, or Black Wealth Deity.

The practice of the Wealth Deity Yoga is, of course, for increased benefits. But, the money that is acquired should be used with good will and not for any wicked purpose — otherwise, there will be severe retributions. Money, itself, is neutral; it is man who creates good or bad karma with it.

Students who manage to rid themselves of poverty should practice all the more. They should live frugally and not extravagantly. Besides practicing the Wealth Deity Yoga, they must practice the Personal Deity Yoga daily, knowing that the most meaningful thing in life is to practice for liberation. It is not to make money and become millionaires.

Among the students, there are, unfortunately, many who are greedy. They wish to get something for nothing. They do not work hard, yet they hope money will be easy to come by. These students wear the *jackpot winning charm* and actively practice the Wealth Deity Yoga. However, they are neither sincere nor honestly desperate. They only have the rich man's dream. Such students are not practical; they always want to be lucky. The deities will not grant their luck. Although the charm is efficacious, without the blessing from the deities, it will not send forth its magical power.

At present, many students send numbers to me for my blessings. However, there is only one grand prize winner and there are more than three hundred requests sent to me every month. Therefore, I can only let Heaven decide who's going to win.

Many students are excessive in their requests. They

want to win every time when they play mahjong or dice and, when they go to Las Vegas or Reno to gamble, they want to win big. Despite the great fortune with which Master can endow students, careful considerations have to be made too.

In Indonesia, there is a student who used to be very poor and lived in a rented house. Working daily in a rubber plantation, he earned very small wages. But, he never stopped reciting the Guru's Heart Mantra. He had a photograph of the Master enlarged and framed. To the photo he added a white lotus seat and an aura around the head, making it more magnificent. Every night, before he went to sleep, he would take the photo from a bag and do his practice; when he was done, he put it away in the bag again.

One day, he dreamed of the Master giving him a shining lottery ticket. He had never bought a ticket before but, inspired by the dream, he bought one. It turned out to be a first prize winner. Winning this first prize turned him into a rich man.

Today, he has not forgotten the source of his fortune. In the middle of his Tantric altar there is a statue of the Padmakumara; on the right is the statue of Buddha Shakyamuni and on the left is the Four Armed Kuan Yin Bodhisattva. He places wreaths of white flowers around all the pictures of deities. Now, he has also set up the Eight Offerings, which makes the altar look more dignified. The spiritual energy around it is strong.

This Indonesian student is Lian-lu of Surabaya.

Lian-lu's dream about the Master unexpectedly changed him from a poor worker into a rich man. This is a true incident. Lian-lu is blessed because he chants the Guru Heart Mantra and pays homage, with utmost respect, to the picture of Master. Padmakumara has bestowed protection as well as a great fortune on him. This was another miracle of the Holy Red Crown Vajra Master.

There are others. In Malaysia, there was another student who won a first prize ticket.

6. Escape From The Inferno Of Death

Since the English publication of one of my spiritual books, multitudes of Western students have come to take refuge. One of them is a Mr. Raymond, an international trade businessman. His company mailing address in Seattle is P.O.Box 738, Seattle, Washington 98111.[1] He had previously learned Kalika and was introduced to me by Doctor Chieh Wen. Mr. Raymond then took refuge in the Holy Red Crown Vajra Master Sheng-yen Lu, the Venerable Tantric Practitioner.

In January, 1985, Mr. Raymond came to say goodbye to me before leaving the country to do business overseas. At that time, I gave him a Dharma picture of mine and a copper amulet and told him that he could chant the Guru Heart Mantra anywhere, at any time. I also told him he could take out the Master's picture and practice the Guru Yoga during his trip.

Mr. Raymond asked me if this journey was inauspicious.

I did an aura reading on him and replied, "You will have a frightening experience in Southeast Asia. However, once it is over, everything will go smoothly for you." I specially told him that the Master's spiritual light would protect him at all times, and that he should be afraid of nothing.

On the night, February 13th, 1985, Mr. Raymond

---

[1] This was the mailing address of Mr. Raymond in 1985.

was in his room on the third floor of the Regent Hotel in Manila. At nine o'clock, he took out the Master's Dharma picture and did his practice. He went to bed at ten. At about eleven o'clock he saw the Master in his dream, wearing a yellow robe and a yellow hat, and smiling at him.

In his dream, Mr. Raymond asked the Master, "Aren't you in the United States? Why are you here in Manila?"

"I've specially come to see you, Lian-piao." (Mr. Raymond's refuge name is Lian-piao.)

"It is a long journey! I am very grateful to you for doing that."

"Do you remember that prior to your departure, I told you that you will have a frightening experience in Southeast Asia?"

"Yes, I do. I do. I do."

"Now, it's time to get up, now it's time to get up, hurry, hurry, ..."

Master shook Lian-piao vigorously with his hands and Lian-piao was like a boat being rocked violently back and forth by the wind and tides. Still in his dream, Lian-piao continued to murmur, "Master, please do not shake, do not shake..."

Then suddenly he woke up. There was no Master. It was a dream. But the dialogue in the dream alerted him. He got up and checked the time — it was eleven-thirty p.m.. Mr. Raymond opened the door. There was thick smoke outside. Instinctively, he put on his clothes, grabbed his briefcase, rushed down the stairs and, in no time, was out on the street. By this time, the fire was burning ferociously in the hotel. Mr. Raymond stood on the spot, terrified. For a moment this, too, felt like a dream.

The fire at Manila's Regent Hotel began in two

places. One was in the conference room on the second floor, the other was in a room on the ninth floor. The fires started at around eleven-thirty p.m., and quickly spread throughout the hotel. Damage was extremely serious.

There were twenty-two identified dead, uncountable numbers of injured, and many unidentified bodies. Among the dead were two Americans: Edward Carroll, a U.S. Internal Revenue Service official based in Tokyo, and Lewis Carrol Rowney, a serviceman stationed at Subic Bay Naval Base.

Mr. Raymond saw a woman standing on the eighth floor's balcony crying, "Help! Help me please!" But, no one moved, because nobody could help her. Many people jumped to their deaths. Some were killed by sharp, broken glass, some hit protruding blocks and broke their limbs. It was cruel to watch.

The huge fire, people escaping, suffocating, burning, and jumping off the building interwove in a living tragedy. People become totally helpless in such a situation. Inside a third-floor room, three people, hugging together, were burned to charcoal.

Mr. Raymond felt extreme sorrow, but he was grateful that he was completely unharmed. He even had his valuable briefcase in his hands. He wholeheartedly believes that the Master is a Buddha, a Bodhisattva whose works of miracles are not myths, not absurdities, and not groundless.

Mr. Raymond said that the wisdom of Master is very rare. It was the Light of the Master that woke him up in the dream. From the United States, a ray of Light emitted by the Master traveled thousands of miles to reach Manila — this is an act of omnipresence. Mr. Raymond is grateful for his second chance in life and believes that the practice of the Guru Yoga and the chanting of the Guru Heart Mantra have ultimately saved his life.

Mr. Raymond's account of this true incident proves the great power of Padmakumara. Padmakumara is a Bodhisattva from the Pure Land of Amitabha Buddha, and a Great Energy of the Universe. This is an era of salvation by Padmakumara. Vajra Master Sheng-yen Lu is only one of the many transformations of Padmakumara, incarnated in a human body in order to help release the world's beings from suffering and misery.

The events recorded in this book, *The Mystical Experiences of True Buddha Disciples*, are fact. They are absolutely not fantastic "myths." One should know that the number of people helped and saved by the Master has reached tens of thousands.

Many people might wonder how Vajra Master Sheng-yen Lu is capable of making multiple appearances to help his disciples. As a matter of fact, I have explained this many times before. During the course of cultivation, one can, in the state of meditation, concentrate the power of the mind and unite it with the Great Energy of the Supreme Consciousness of the Universe. If one can do this, one will possess the power of the Great Energy, the Great Energy of meditation and wisdom.

To say one possesses the Great Energy of meditation and wisdom is equivalent to saying that, by applying the energy of the weak magnetic field of our human body, one can command the energy of the strong magnetic field of the Universe. You and the Universe become one and, when you think of doing something, the Great Energy of the Universe will do it for you, as if you were doing it yourself. It is like radiations beaming reciprocally at each other. This is supernatural and exceedingly powerful.

I knew beforehand that Lian-piao would be in a frightening predicament.

However, as he always chanted the Guru Heart Mantra and practiced the Guru Yoga, I knew he was in tune all the time with the Great Energy of Padmakumara.

When disaster fell on Lian-piao, the Great Energy of Padmakumara manifested in the form of the Master to save him. Therefore, he escaped the inferno of death.

The same logic applies to *sincerely chanting the name of the Buddha.* If one does this, one is thinking of the Buddha all the time. The Buddha knows about you because you always call upon him. Then, when you are in trouble, the Buddha will know and manifest to rescue you. Many people practice the Pure Land [method] by chanting the name of Amitabha Buddha until the mind becomes concentrated and singly focused on Amitabha. For the same reason as before, the Buddhas and Bodhisattvas will appear and rescue the practitioners. This is *rebirth in the Pure Land through chanting Amitabha.*

7. Voices Through The Walls

There is a student whose refuge name is "Lian-chung."
(In this chapter only his refuge name will be used as it has
impact on other people.) Lian-chung was the manager of
a Taipei trading company. Business in the company was
very smooth and lucrative. Three acquaintances involved
in the same trade invited Lian-chung into a joint-venture
in setting up another large, trading company.

Lian-chung is a very prudent person. Whenever he
starts a new venture, he writes to consult with the Master before making his decisions. Therefore, his business
thrives and he has never had any loss. Naturally, he wrote
to the Master regarding the joint-venture of this new company.

After the letter was mailed and before Lian-chung
received any reply, the other three partners invited him
to discuss the plan of the new venture at the offices of
another company. This other company was located on
the second floor of a building in which Mr. Chang, the
person in charge of the company, had a residence on the
ninth floor.

After long hours of discussion, Lian-chung felt tired
and wanted to leave. But the trio would not let him go,
suggesting that they all go out for supper at the end of
the meeting. Mr. Chang proposed that Lian-chung first
take a rest in the guest room of his residence on the ninth
floor. Later they would call him for supper.

Lian-chung went upstairs to Mr. Chang's residence
and fell fast asleep. Sometime later, he woke suddenly.

36

Something strange was happening — he unexpectedly heard the voices of his three partners talking about plans. The voices were tiny, but extremely clear. It was very quiet in the guest room except for the voices that went on continuously. Lian-chung knew positively the voices were those of his partners. He heard everything they said.

"This time when he joins us, we will take care of him together."

"Chang will be responsible for all the controls and will bring him down."

"Ha! We will definitely get rid of him this time."

He heard many plans. For example: to use his checks to draw cash; to arrange for one of Chang's relatives to take care of the accounting; how to give misleading quotations; how to make empty promises; how to secure the actual controls; and how to cheat. The more Lian-chung heard, the more shocked he was. He tried to pinch himself, to see if it were a dream, but he could definitely feel the pain. Hurriedly he put on his clothes and took the elevator from the ninth floor down to the second floor conference room, where the trio was still meeting.

Lian-chung was perplexed to see them there. How had he been able to hear their voices from where he had been sleeping so many floors away? Wasn't this strange? Between the second and ninth floor were many floors and ceilings. Could he have experienced the Faculty of the **Divine Hearing**?

In disbelief, he asked, "When I was asleep, did anyone go up to the ninth floor?"

"No," they answered together. "We were here all the time, did someone wake you?"

"No," Lian-chung replied. "Tell me, has the accountant been selected?"

"It's Mr. Wu, who is my distant relative," Chang replied. "He is very capable, responsible and reliable."

Lian-chung had already heard this when he was on the ninth floor. Now, back on the second floor, the answers matched. Nevertheless, he was shocked.

When Lian-chung went home, he lit an incense on his altar, in the middle of which was enshrined a porcelain statue of the Holy Red Crown Vajra Master. He then reported everything to the Master, and chanted the Guru Heart Mantra and practiced the Guru Yoga. Lian-chung believed he was able to hear the plot against him because he had enshrined the Master's porcelain statue in his altar and, unknowingly, he was protected by an invisible force, the Great Energy of Padmakumara of the Western Paradise. Undoubtedly, the Bodhisattva was protecting him, opening his divine ears at the right time; otherwise, he could not have heard the secret conversation.

As a matter of fact, Lian-chung had intended to join the new business. It would have been a very serious blow to him if the three other partners were going to cheat him. That could have led to the loss of his wealth or even his life.

He shuddered and was appalled by the ugly heart of people. It reminded him of the incident when the original name of the school founded by Master was stolen by a group of shameless people. Lian-chung had worked very hard all his life for his trading company and it could all have been lost. Thinking of this, he held the incense, and thanked the Master over and over again for the mystical experience.

Since then, Lian-chung has sincerely chanted the Guru Heart Mantra one thousand eighty times daily, even when he is walking, standing, sitting, or lying down. He feels that Holy Red Crown Vajra Master is miraculous and very compassionate.

Shortly thereafter, Master's reply arrived in the mail; it was just a few simple but clear verses:

Beware of fraudulence this time,
Let not prosperity wither out;
Divinity will alert you,
Everything will become clear in the future.

Having read the verses, Lian-chung was deeply touched. He immediately wrote a letter to the Master, detailing everything and his decision not to join the new business, so as to avoid entrapment and ruin. Later, according to a report from Lian-chung, the trio got another innocent person to go in with them and they did away with him using the same methods they had discussed using on Lian-chung.

Lian-chung once related this mystical experience to an eminent monk. The eminent monk said that it was absolutely possible for someone to experience a temporary Divine Hearing due to the intervention of Bodhisattvas. It was the power of the Bodhisattvas that had transported the voices of the conspiring trio to Lian-chung's ears, so that he could make the right decisions regarding his future.

This eminent monk further affirmed that Vajra Master Sheng-yen Lu is actually the transformation of a great Bodhisattva who uses very special methods to salvage sentient beings; it is just that ordinary cultivators do not quite understand him yet. Vajra Master Lian-shen's knowledge of mystical Dharmas is enormous. He is a great Bodhisattva who would sacrifice himself to save sentient beings, which is very rare in our contemporary era.

This eminent monk is Lian-chung's teacher in the Sutrayana School. Lian-chung has, altogether, four teachers, all of whom are quite well-known.

8. A Case of Instantaneous Transportation

Readers who watch television will know of the Star Trek series about a spaceship that carries its captain and crew into all kinds of inter-planetary adventures.

Viewers know that, when the captain and crew want to visit a planet, they do not have to land the spaceship on it. Instead, they enter a "transporter" and, after exposure to a de-materializing energy beam, they disappear and gradually re-materialize on the planet.

To return to the spaceship, the procedure works the same way. By standing in one spot, after contacting the spaceship, they "beam up," de-materializing from the planet and re-materializing back in the transporter. Star Trek is, of course, science fiction. Nevertheless, we can't deny that many kinds of science fiction have become reality. In fact, this Universe is so boundlessly enormous that every planet or star has its own mystery, beyond humanity's wildest dreams.

I had a strange encounter that I particularly noted down because it was a truly extraordinary case of "transporting."

At twelve noon, Sunday, February 17th, 1985, my wife Li-hsiang Lu and I, and our two children, Fo-ch'ing and Fo-ch'i, drove from Redmond, where we had had hamburgers at a local McDonald's restaurant, to a big department store in Bellevue which was, at that time, having a furniture sale.

In the United States, sales are often the best way

to attract customers. There are car sales, home sales, furniture sales, fashion sales, etc.. Whenever there is a sale, stores are jam-packed with people and the parking lots are always full as well.

That day, the parking lot was full and many cars were cruising around for a space to park. To get a parking space depends on the timing. When a car is just about to leave a space, one must position oneself so that one can drive quickly into the space the moment it is vacated. Sometimes one can drive around for hours and not find a space to park, so the parking problem is serious.

I drove straight into the parking lot (please note that it was the first level of the parking lot that I entered). I couldn't find a space and so I turned left, and moved straight ahead a short distance. The ground was level; there were no slopes at all. I still did not see any space, so I chanted the mantra "Om Mani Padme Hum" once. Suddenly a car was backing out of a stall right in front of us! I was glad. At last we had found a parking spot, and my wife and children applauded as we pulled into the space.

Once we got out of the car, we were puzzled. We assumed we were on the first level, but there were people walking below. I looked again. We were parked on the second floor!

"Did I drive up the ramp to the second floor just now?" I asked.

"No!"

"That's right, I remember very clearly. We went straight into the first level, turned left and stopped. We did not go up any ramp. How could this be the second floor?"

My wife was also surprised. We walked once around the floor and found there was no ramp connecting level one and level two. To go to level two from level one, it was necessary to go to the rear entrance and up a spiral ramp. I knew absolutely that I had not entered from the rear entrance, nor did I drive up a spiral ramp, so how could the car end up on level two?

I again checked the pillars in the car park; the words "second level" were plainly written on them. Looking down from level two I could see many cars going in and out of the level one entrance we had just driven through. My question was, how could we be on level two instead of level one? Not only was I surprised, but so was my wife. She also knew that it was not possible to reach level two by the route we had taken.

It was like a dream — in an instant the first level became the second level! This happened in broad daylight, and the shift took place in the blinking of an eye. It was a very real and instant transportation, a joke created by the Buddhas and Bodhisattvas.

I think this was how it happened: the Buddhas and Bodhisattvas followed us to the department store in Bellevue. They took a look, and saw that level one was full but that a car was moving out on level two. They did not inform us in time and so, with a disassociation method, they de-materialized us and the car into formless energy, which rose up to the second level. They then put us back again with the re-materialization method. This de-materializing and re-materializing was done in an instant, the very instant when I chanted "Om Mani Padme Hum."

The space travelers in the science fiction series, Star Trek, utilized the "de-materialization" and "re-materialization" method of traveling back and forth between their spaceship and the planets. In an instant, as in a dream, positions are shifted. That day, the four of us, together with the car, also experienced such instantaneous transportation, going from level one to level two. It was indeed wonderful!

In the Amitabha Sutra expounded by Buddha Shakyamuni, there is a verse: "At this time, Lord Buddha addressed the elder Subhuti: To the west, passing one hundred thousand billion of Buddha-lands, there is a world called Ultimate Bliss [Sukhavati], where there is a Buddha named Amitabha, now expounding the **Buddhadharma**." How far is a hundred thousand billion Buddha-lands? As each Buddha-land is divided into Pure Land, Impure Land, the Land of Reward and the Land of Dharma Nature, these hundred thousand billion Buddha-lands are, of course, not on our planet Earth, but very far away on the planets of another dimension.

Chanting Amitabha to rebirth in Pure Land is actually an *instantaneous transportation.* If a person on Earth constantly chants the name of Amitabha of the faraway Western Paradise, visualizes Amitabha's magnificent Pure Land, and concentrates his mind to one-pointedness, when he dies, a lotus will blossom in the Western Paradise. (*As the lotus blossoms, you will see the Buddha.*) So, when this person dies on Earth, his or her wisdom consciousness will pass through the hundred thousand billion Buddha-lands and will instantly, through transportation, achieve a rebirth in the Pure Land.

The Holy Red Crown Vajra Master Lian-shen, the Tantrika, is the transformation body of Padmakumara of the Maha Twin Lotus Ponds. He also came to testify on behalf of Amitabha. The merits of Amitabha are excellent. His magnificent Pure Land Pathway enables one to be reborn in paradise by traveling instantaneously through the hundred thousand billion Buddha-lands. Such "transporting" is indeed a spectacular manifestation of the Buddha power.

This kind of transporting, shifting both people and car from the first level to the second level, is comparatively a rather insignificant feat, unworthy of causing anyone alarm. But then, in this world where spectacular, magical illusion is rare, it can perhaps be considered an unusual interlude.

9. Lawyer Henry's Daughter

The first lawyer with whom I became acquainted in the United States was Lawyer Henry. His full name is Henry Liebman. He is an earnest lawyer. When I was in the process of obtaining my U.S. immigration visa, he went to Taiwan from the States, especially to help me at the American Institute in Taiwan.

In 1982, on June 16th, my whole family arrived at the Seattle Airport. Lawyer Henry was there to help us through immigration.

Lawyer Henry is of Jewish ancestry. His grandfather had traveled all over the world and had been to China. His father, who was also a lawyer, immigrated to the States and settled down in Miami. When Henry was young, he studied hard and resolved to become a great lawyer. Eventually he succeeded in becoming a lawyer. In addition, he is also an accountant. Therefore he has two careers.

I discovered that there are three kinds of indispensable people in the United States: lawyers, accountants and doctors. These people are needed everywhere, especially the lawyers. In America, lawsuits can happen anytime, anywhere; people are used to going to court even for trivial matters. Therefore, lawyers are definitely needed.

Take for example the construction of Ling Shen Ching Tze Rey Tseng Temple in Redmond. Lawyer Henry acted on our behalf in court to debate the city government and local residents. We went through many court debates, trying to win through legal means the right to establish a Chinese temple. It took three years before approval for the construction was granted. The bitterness we encountered was impossible for someone, who was not involved in it, to understand. Lawyer Henry, however, was able to utilize his strength at the proper moment in the court hearings.

Lawyer Henry helped us and we also helped him. We helped him with his daughter. About six months after she was born, doctors discovered some abnormalities. She frequently and suddenly lost consciousness. This happened without any provocation. Her whole body would become flaccid, sometimes her mouth drooled and her eyes rolled up, which was very frightening.

Henry and his wife had taken her for examinations to all the large hospitals in Seattle. The answers were discouraging:

1) Incurable — the brain was oxygen-deficient.

2) Not going to survive.

3) Even if she survived, she would be mentally retarded.

These were the results of the diagnoses by doctors in the large hospitals.

During this period of time, Lawyer Henry looked wan and worried. He simply could not concentrate on his work and the smile on his face disappeared.

I asked him, "Do you believe in Chinese deities? Do you believe in Chinese charms? Certain Chinese mystical power can save life from death. I believe I can help you, especially since you are our lawyer."

Our American friend, Lawyer Henry, wearing a long face, accepted my offer since he had no other alternative.

At that time, some people had advised me not to write charms to Americans because they simply do not understand the Chinese charms, which involve the drawing of some character-like symbols in ink with a brush-pen. These are drawn on a yellow piece of paper, which is then taken to cure sickness. Americans will not believe it will cure sickness. To help people, I was advised to not use charms but to use, instead, the Great Compassion Dharani Holy Water (water empowered by mantra). In this way, Americans would not criticize it.

But, when Lawyer Henry was at my place, the Buddhas and Bodhisattvas wanted me to draw three charms which were the divine endowment charms. The Bodhisattvas held my hand to draw them and I asked that the Divine Light be empowered on the charms. As a result, three beams of white light radiated from the heavens and shone on the charms for a long time.

After that, I instructed Lawyer Henry to burn one charm every night in a bowl, pour boiled water over the ashes, and filter the water with a coffee filter. Then he must let his daughter drink the water before she went to sleep. I told him to do that each night for three nights and that, in a week, we would see how she had improved. (During this week, I empowered his daughter every night in my practices.)

After a week, the "non-viable" and "mentally retarded" daughter's episodes of fainting decreased. Her eyes did not roll up any more and her mouth no longer drooled. One month later, there was no more loss of consciousness. Lawyer Henry's daughter had become absolutely normal.

The couple again took their daughter to the doctors for complete examinations. The results were that she was cured "miraculously." The brain was no longer oxygen-deficient. The doctors in the big hospitals said "it was impossible." The fact is, the impossible had already become the possible. The doctors were baffled.

On March 5th, 1985, at 7:00 p.m., Lawyer Henry

and Mr. John W. Austin, Vice Cabinet Minister of the Economic Department of the State of Washington, dined with us at the Yu Yuan Restaurant. Lawyer Henry told the Minister the story of his daughter, and the Minister kept saying that it was a miracle.

This is a true story about using three charms to heal Lawyer Henry's daughter, whose brain was oxygen-deficient. Since I arrived in the States, I have also cured many Westerners with mantras and charms. Some of them had insomnia, which was cured in one week. One American woman had a relaxed colon illness; she could not hold her bowel whenever she ate. She had been to many doctors but their treatments were ineffective. She was cured with paper charms within two months and her health returned to normal. She also came to take refuge in the Holy Red Crown Vajra Master.

There was also an administrative officer at the White House in Washington, D.C. who had early stage lung cancer. He was so worried that, in a very short time, his hair turned gray. He came to see me on someone's recommendation. I chanted the Great Compassion Dharani one hundred eight times every day for seven days to bless the water, and then gave it to him in a container. Three months later, he overcame the grave illness and wrote to thank me.

Many Westerners came to take refuge in the Holy Red Crown Vajra Master because their chronic ailments had been cured by the Master. Every Saturday night they attend the Dharma talks given by Master in his house, and they practice meditation together. The occasions are full of Dharma joys, with new concepts and changes of attitude. Everyone bows to the Master after receiving the teachings.

Some of these people have great understanding of the Buddhist teachings. They have gradually eliminated the view of Western supremacy and the idea of the Christian God being the only God. I especially would like to choose from among my Western disciples those who have the quality of a master, teach them the unexcelled fine Dharmas so that they can preach with the power of unhindered discourse.

Among the Western disciples, there will, in the future, be a few great masters who will know the boundlessness of Buddha Dharma, the limitlessness of Buddha power, and have deep understanding of the Dharma.

The main task of the emergence of Western masters is to help the Westerners.

10. Seeking One's Fate

When I was in Taiwan, a high school teacher came to take refuge in me. I gave her the refuge name Lian-lu. Tall and healthy looking, Lian-lu was a beautiful woman. She had long hair, sparkling and fascinating eyes, and a high-bridged nose. With a good job and a sweet face, one would think that she would have no problem in making a good marriage.

However, the school where she was teaching was a girls' school and she had only a few male colleagues. Besides, Lian-lu's standards were on the high side. She did not care for any of the men to whom she had been introduced. Thus she was unsuccessful in one way or another. Her marriage did not materialize.

Once Lian-lu came to ask me when and where would her marriage occur? Using my divination method, I checked carefully for her but, after several tries, was still unable to get a solid answer. It all looked very uncertain and distant. I told her honestly, there seemed to be no settling place for her in the world.

"Does that mean I have to become a nun?" She asked sadly, showing a row of white teeth.

"Not so," I replied.

"Master! What should I do? Please, check for me once more."

This time, as I concentrated again and checked once more I saw a Japanese-made porcelain statue of Kuan-yin Bodhisattva, dressed in a kimono. It was the Kuan-yin that Lian-lu worshiped at home which was consecrated by me. This Kuan-yin Bodhisattva told me that Lian-lu's fate was in America.

"America?" She gasped, amazed.

"Yes, Bodhisattva said so."

"It's impossible Master; I have no relatives in America and no reason to go there. At present, my chance of going overseas to study is zero. I have never thought of going to America," she said.

"But Bodhisattva, indeed, said so!"

In the summer of 1982, I immigrated to America. Lian-lu had not been in touch with me. She had not even written a letter to me. Then, in the summer of 1983, she sent me a card and a short note, "Master, I am taking an opportunity this summer vacation to tour the United States and I will pay the Master a visit in Seattle."

That summer, I met Lian-lu at my old residence, the Ling Shen Attic. Wearing fashionable Western apparel, earrings and boots, she still looked very pretty.

"Master, I have come!"

I was very glad to see her, too.

"Master, read my fate again. I am here in America!"

I carefully did a reading for her. Vaguely, I saw an ugly old man, his back slightly humped, his nose red, a Westerner of sixty or more years. When I saw this scene, I was surprised, but told Lian-lu exactly what happened.

"Do I have to marry this strange old man?" asked Lian-lu dejectedly.

I was silent.

The way things turned out surprised everyone. Lian-lu's female companion for the trip had to leave the States earlier than planned. While Lian-lu was dining alone in a restaurant, an old Westerner came and requested to share the table with her. The old man was indeed slightly humpbacked and had a red nose. He was not handsome but very kind and friendly. The old man liked Lian-lu very much and they talked a lot. Lian-lu did not like him in the beginning, but discovered that he was very humorous and kind, so she was very happy to chat with him.

The old man took Lian-lu on a tour of the scenic spots and they became good friends, despite the great difference in age. The old man was sixty-four years old and Lian-lu was thirty.

"Master, you mean I have to marry this old man?"

"I am not sure, but you have indeed met him," I replied.

"My god! This is really my fate, an America fate?"

One day, the old man introduced Lian-lu to his son, who was a professor at a university in Arizona. He was thirty six years old and unmarried. His name was LoLa. Once introduced, LoLa immediately fell in love with Lian-lu, and Lian-lu liked LoLa, too. Both seemed to fall in love with each other at first sight.

Now, Lian-lu finally was going to get married.

They became engaged and were going back to Arizona to get married. LoLa was still teaching at the Arizona university.

The old man was very happy with his son's choice of a wife.

Lian-lu said, "Master's divine reading is really amazing."

"It is a good thing that he didn't turn out to be the Hunchback of Notre Dame," I teased her. And she was overwhelmed with joy.

Lian-lu originally held a six-month tourist visa. She believed the Master's words, but she was aware of the slim chance of meeting her predestined husband in the vast populace of a country as huge as the United States. But, strange encounter and unexpected fate did indeed happen. This was truly a fated marriage.

The marriage effectively altered her status from a tourist into a permanent resident, and very soon she would get her citizenship.

A divine reading I made in my homeland of Taiwan finally became realized several years later overseas. This was unmistakably the guidance of the divine lights of Buddhas and Bodhisattvas. Such a miraculous prediction and wonderful encounter are achievable by the Holy Red Crown Vajra Master Sheng-yen Lu, the Tantrika. Lian-lu's realization of her marriage is great evidence.

The divine reading of the Holy Red Crown Vajra Master is renowned all over the world. Recently, there were people from Europe, Singapore and Taiwan who flew over just to ask a single question, then flew back the next day. This is extraordinary.

I wrote a verse for Lian-lu:

The wonderful reading of Master amazes again,
Displaying supernatural powers at home and over-
*   seas;*
Intricately fate brings the persons together, just like
*   what happens in a drama,*
And finally love comes her way.

11. Rescue in Secrecy

The Holy Red Crown Vajra Master Lian-shen, with his unlimited spiritual power, has already undertaken to rescue many people in secrecy. The wonderful Master has already obtained the approval of the many Buddhas, numbering in the ninety-nine billions of Ganges sands, and has the ability to emit the great light of the Tathagata. In the course of rescuing people, the Master has manifested in numerous division bodies. His Heart Mantra represents all the great secret mantras, turning the great Dharma Wheel during his meditations. His transformations are many and have already filled up the Universe. There are also uncountable dragons (**Nagas**), devas, and gods that help him in spreading the Dharma. Maras escape upon seeing his lights. The Holy Red Crown Vajra Master Lian-shen is able to travel freely throughout the Buddha kingdoms and the nether world. His manifestations have already extended into the non-physical realms.

Here is a record of a non-physical rescue.

One day, after taking ablution, I entered the True Buddha Tantric Quarter, lit an incense and chanted the Thousand-armed and Thousand-eyed Great Compassion Heart Dharani. After chanting the Dharani seven times, I suddenly saw the Thousand-armed and Thousand-eyed Avalokitesvara Bodhisattva appearing, with light shining from one of the hands that form the *willow branch holding mudra*. This *willow branch holding* hand signifies the riddance of all kinds of illnesses of the body. While I was amazed, the index finger of this hand suddenly pointed towards the ground.

All of a sudden, I found myself in the nether world. Although in the nether world, I was still suspended in space, being enveloped by a gentle, auspicious light being emitted from my whole body.

I saw many spirit-guards running to and fro. I saw those who had descended to the nether world were suffering from "frying," "sawing," "snake bites," and "burning." They cried painfully. It was cruel to watch. One of the kings of the nether world, sitting high up and looking stern, was leafing through a registry. Suddenly, he cried out, "Arrest 'XXX' quickly and bring him here." Upon hearing this, the two spirit-guards on each side made ready to leave the palace.

As soon as I heard it was "XXX", I knew he was my student. I was astonished, and quickly folded my palms and respectfully asked the nether world king, "Your majesty, wasn't that my student 'XXX' you just mentioned?"

"That is the right person."

With the auspicious light protecting me, I moved towards the desk this time and saw that the records on the registry detailing the stated time of my student's death was between 9.00 p.m. and 11:00 p.m., on the 19th day of the seventh month of the lunar calendar, at forty-eight years of age. I folded my palms and spoke to the king respectfully. "This student has not done any bad deeds in his life and is practicing the Tantra very diligently. In the future, he is going to do the work of salvation and will be the backbone of our school. If he dies, he will not fulfill his wish. Please grant him a pardon!"

"Venerable Lian-shen, this registry is the secret order of the highest commander of the nether world. I would not dare to take the matter in my own hands to release him, unless there is a special reason," the king said.

At this time, the king ordered the scribe at his side to check again into the merits of "XXX." As a result, they found out that he had recently talked ten people into taking refuge in the True Buddha School, persuaded people to practice cultivation and to chant the Guru Heart Mantra, the Great Compassion Dharani and the names of Buddhas and Bodhisattvas.

The king was delighted, "Give him another twelve years of life according to these merits!"

I was also glad to hear that!

From the nether world, I returned to my True Buddha Tantric Quarter and emerged from my meditation.

Soon thereafter I received a letter from "XXX" which said:

In the seventh month of the lunar calendar, I suddenly felt unusually fatigued, my whole body sweated, my mouth was dry, and dark circles appeared around my eyes. The doctors who checked me said I was in kidney failure. I had many weird dreams at night and my energy level was low during the day. I felt like collapsing when I walked and my back ached.

Even when my body was very weak, I did not forget to bow to the Kuan Yin Bodhisattva every day, recite the Universal Gateway Article of the Lotus Sutra, recite the Guru Heart Mantra and pray for the help of Master and Bodhisattvas. Despite having seen many doctors and having had many medications, I did not get well. Instead, I came down with a high fever that would not recede.

Following a Tantric teaching Master had previously taught me, I practiced the Willow Hand Yoga every day continuously for a week. At the beginning, being sick, I had to struggle to finish with it, and the illness did not get better; it seemed to be getting worse and worse.

One night, sometime after the middle of the seventh month of the lunar year, I saw Master in a dream and Master gave me a bowl of medicine to drink. Suddenly, I felt completely recovered from the illness. From then on I got better, recuperating gradually. The prescribed medications started to work well too. I was overjoyed.

I did not write to Master for a long time due to this illness which I went through. From now on, I will take special care of my health, because health is the prerequisite for spreading the Dharma of the True Buddha School. Master always taught us to look after both our health and our mind. This illness has given me a great revelation. Thank you Master for your protection.

This was the letter of "XXX."

His letter proved all that I had seen. Undoubtedly, he had escaped death this time. This is the advantage of taking refuge, practicing meditation, and performing charitable deeds. In my reply to his letter, I did not mention what I had seen. As a matter of fact, I did not save him. He saved himself.

There are many illnesses that are related to "cause and effect" and "karma." Doctors may not be able to cure these kinds of karmic sicknesses. There are many strange illnesses for which doctors are not able to find causes.

I advise students that it is necessary to see doctors. In addition, however, students must also cultivate their minds and bodies, and perform more good deeds, (such as reciting the powerful Thousand-armed and Thousand-eyed Great Compassion Heart Dharani). Drinking the Great Compassion Dharani Water also generates many inconceivable miracles. These kinds of psychic responses are too numerous to be mentioned.

The Holy Red Crown Vajra Master Lian-shen believes that all Buddhas and Bodhisattvas have great compassion and loving kindness, possess all supernatural powers and, in response, will secretly come to the help of those who are in danger. For Buddhas and Bodhisattvas to come to your rescue, it is necessary to sincerely pray and to recite their names and mantras. There will be a response. I know the sufferings of sentient beings are incessant. To have Buddhas and Bodhisattvas help in response, it is necessary to have great sincerity and to learn to become a Bodhisattva. Then if one is in danger, Bodhisattvas will respond and come to help.

If one is without sincerity, Bodhisattvas will not respond.

If one is without kindness, Bodhisattvas will not respond.

For the same reason, if students of True Buddha School want to receive responses from the master, they must be "sincere" and "kind." The combination of these two qualities will enable students to receive responses.

The Guru Heart Mantra, a great Dharani, emits great light like the great sun. This Heart Mantra contains great compassion, supernatural power, light of the Ten Directions, equal salvation, and the Pure Land of the Buddha. The Guru's Mantra is inconceivable and those who recite it two hundred thousand times are the ones who have great affinity with the Western Paradise of Ultimate Bliss. They will all be saved.

12. A Strange Ghostly Look

Doctors treat sickness but, if there is not sickness, doctors can do nothing.

Is a "strange ghostly look" a sickness or not?

I have a new student in Southeast Asia whose refuge name is Lian-fu.

This chapter may affect the marriage of a girl; therefore, the name of the country involved will not be mentioned, nor will the girl's real name. Instead, I will use a fictitious name for this girl, "Hui-yin." Hui-yin is the daughter of Lian-fu.

Hui-yin is already a graduate of the university. I have a picture of her wearing her cap and gown at her baccalaureate graduation. She has fine, silky hair, prominent eyebrows and pretty eyes. She looks intelligent and healthy.

But Lian-fu told me that he had a secret worry which was also the worry of the whole family.

No one knew how it started but, ever since she was very young, every morning when Hui-yin woke up, she always made a weird gesture in which she stuck out her tongue, rolled her eyes up, and stretched both her arms out in front as if she were going to strangle someone.

This gesture was just like ones little children make to scare people. Generally, people assume children are just being naughty when they do this. But, it was different in Hui-yin's case because, when she did it, her face looked strange and ghostly. She wasn't faking anything and she would only wake up when she was slapped. At first she didn't even know of her strange, waking gesture and she did not understand why she did it.

This didn't happen just for one or two days, nor for one or two months, but every day from the time she was quite young until she graduated from the university. Each day she did the same kind of ghostly gestures. Her parents took her to see doctors, but she was completely healthy and there was nothing abnormal with her brain waves. Of course she would not respond to any kind of medical treatment.

So every morning, right after Hui-yin woke up, she stuck out her tongue, rolled up her eyes, and stretched out her arms. Her parents felt extremely sad. They did everything they could think of to make her stop — even scolding and beating her. But it wasn't Hui-yin's fault.

In the area where they lived, there were many Buddhist temples and many witch-doctors. Lian-fu went to many Buddhist masters, who helped him by reciting repentance sutras. He also tried Taoist teachers and witch-doctors — anything that seemed to have magical powers, but it didn't help. Hui-yin remained the same.

When Lian-fu took refuge in me, he gave me her graduation picture and date of birth, and begged me to help.

So, I set up an altar for remote-healing and, after taking ablution, went to practice. I gave his daughter a remote-empowerment with the "Divine (Triple Hum) Water."

Three days into my practice, a miraculous thing happened. That night, when I was visualizing Lian-fu's daughter, her spirit came. I scanned her and found there was a stain, a red streak of blood on her neck. Now I understood... her previous life was ...

So, each night for three nights in front of the Buddhas, I sincerely recited, for the duration of the burning of a stick of incense, the Great Compassion Dharani, requesting the Great Compassion Dharani Holy Water. Then, I called upon Hui-yin's spirit and sprinkled the water onto the blood stain on her neck.

After sprinkling water on her for three nights, her spirit became full of vigor and the blood stain disappeared. Her neck completely recovered.

In my letter to Lian-fu, I enclosed three energized charms that I had requested from the Buddhas and Bodhisattvas. I instructed him to burn one per night at bedtime, mix the ash with water, and let his daughter drink the water. With this additional remote healing, Hui-yin was completely cured and normal. No longer each morning did she stick out her tongue, roll up her eyes, and stretch her arms out to strangle people. She was now completely normal. This problem, which had afflicted her since childhood, was gone. Again, this is an evidence of the boundlessness of Buddha Dharma.

I know Lian-fu and his family are believers of the right Buddhist doctrines. However, due to Hui-yin's illness, they had searched all the temples and even resorted to the witchcrafts of the natives. They had acquired many merits from having Buddhist masters chant repentance sutras for them. They went to see many Eastern and Western doctors — the country's well-known doctors, even foreign experts in neurology and psychology — all without results.

Was this an illness? Yes, it was, but not a common illness. It was a "karmic illness."

The Holy Red Crown Vajra Master is one who specializes in curing "karmic illnesses." The miracles displayed by the Master have surprised doctors, many of whom have come to take refuge in him. This is because the Master has actual power, and there are many proven examples in which sick people have been cured.

There was a well-known doctor, an authority, who made a diagnosis on a young patient suffering from cancer of the esophagus. The young patient came to take refuge in me and practiced the Guru Yoga daily. He also drank the Great Compassion Dharani Holy Water and discovered that his esophagus gave out sounds resembling ice cubes melting. After a month or so, he went back to see the famous doctor who was shocked to see that the cancer had disappeared. The doctor asked the young man what had happened.

When the young man told him, the doctor was extremely impressed. He requested to see me. Once he saw me, the doctor knelt down immediately, bowed, and took refuge. The doctor's wife was with him, but she was hesitant to follow her husband's actions. She was finally persuaded by her husband, and knelt down and bowed to the Master.

On the question of prostrating to the Master, I have observed a problem which I want to address briefly here. It is not necessary to prostrate before the Master whenever a student sees him. However, if the student has not seen the Master for a long time, he may prostrate (perform the Great Homage) once, which is good enough. The Master will definitely give a blessing in return, and empower the student with mantras. These are part of the formalities in Tantra.

If you see the Master frequently, folding the palms together should be enough. This is paying respect.

Many students who are government officials, doctors and lawyers, are not used to doing prostration because of their eminent positions. Master will not compel them to do so. Instead, they can just fold their palms together and Master will give a blessing in return. It is not necessary to engage in formalities when paying respect, as long as one has the respect in one's heart. It is better not to compel anyone to follow formalities. This will avoid embarrassment.

13. The Case of A Strange Odor

In early summer 1982, Holy Red Crown Vajra Master Lian-shen arrived in the United States. At that time, students in the States did not know about my arrival and there were not that many U.S. students anyway. So, the Master made prostrations to the Buddhas in the morning and practiced meditation at night, living a quiet and simple life.

Soon, some students living nearby requested teachings, and some others came for guidance. Because of the Dharma joy my students received and the wonderful guidance service I provided, news spread and many more came to listen to the teachings. Since then, whenever there is a teaching, the attendance is always full.

Right now, in America, there are students in Los Angeles, San Francisco, New York, and other places where local chapters are in the planning stages. These initiated students, numbering tens of thousands, all started from the point of believing, and continued through understanding, and on to actual practicing. From there, they help others to understand the teachings, and help the Master to propagate the Dharma. The time is ripe for the joy of Dharma to fill all sentient beings.

This short chapter concerns the psychic experience of a female student.

While the Master was in Seattle, a woman, Mrs. Jung-san Hsueh, took refuge in me. She practiced her meditation very diligently everyday. Her mystical experiences were numerous. During meditation, she saw various strange happenings, yet could remain undisturbed.

After she started her Tantric practice, she had an accident in which her foot was run over by a car, however, the foot wasn't injured; she had a stomach operation and Kuan Yin Bodhisattva appeared before her and healed the incision which became cool and soothing. She received clear guidance from the Bodhisattvas.

Recently, Mrs. Jung-san Hsueh had a very strong psychic experience. Sometime in February, 1985, while at home, she smelled a very strange odor — a very unusual and bad odor. At first, she thought it was just a coincidence. However, the odor did not disappear; instead, it got stronger every day.

She was the only one who could smell it. No one else smelled it. The smell was strong, like something rotten.

Mrs. Hsueh lived in Renton. She had already achieved response from the Guru Yoga and, whenever she invoked the Master through the Guru's Heart Mantra, she could see the Master appearing in lights in her meditation. This time after she invoked him, the Master appeared in an aura of auspicious light. "Master, why is there this strange odor?" Mrs. Hsueh asked.

"Your relative is ill." Master replied and disappeared.

She wondered which relative of hers was sick. Why hadn't she heard anything? So she went into meditation again and saw her father-in-law, then she saw black light coming out of the area of his duodenum. Oh! It's her father-in-law's duodenal ulcer!

She told her husband right away and he immediately called long distance to Kaohsiung, Taiwan, where his father was living.

The couple found out that the family in Taiwan had not wanted to worry them, and therefore had not notified them. And, indeed, during that period of time, Mrs. Hsueh's father-in-law had suffered a hemorrhage from his duodenal ulcer. He had vomited a great deal of blood and had two liters of blood transfused into him. He was sent to the T'sai Surgical Hospital and had been in a coma since the operation. Five days into the coma, the hospital personnel thought he was not going to live and wanted the family to consider the funeral. Upon hearing this over the phone, Mrs. Hsueh was startled and immediately started to practice a healing yoga which the Master had taught her. She continued meditating until she saw a bright white light appearing from the area of his duodenum.

Her father-in-law stayed eighteen days in the hospital. He was in a coma for a week. During this time, the hospital had virtually given up on him. However, instead of dying, he woke up. Resting, over the next ten days in the hospital, he gradually recuperated. This was a miraculous occurrence wherein the dying had begun to live again.

On Sunday, March 10, 1985, Mrs. Hsueh and her husband drove from Renton to my True Buddha Tantric Quarter, for the purpose of requesting me to perform a blessing for their father. They brought along some bread, pastries, fruits, incense and gold decorated papers as offerings to the Buddhas. I lit the candles and recited the Universal Gateway Article of the Lotus Sutra, the High King Avalokitesvara Sutra, and the Six Syllables Mantra "Om Mani Padme Hum." Together with the mudra and visualization, I gave them blessings.

Mrs. Jung-san Hsueh could "see," "hear" and "smell"

in her meditation. She is extremely sincere and is mindful of Kuan Yin Bodhisattva at all times. Thus:

All beings who are in distress,
And in an enormous amount of pain;
The wisdom power of Kuan Yin,
Can save them from all sufferings.

An unusual aspect of Mrs. Hsueh's taking refuge was, ever since she was initiated, she was no longer obsessed with all the worries she had had before and she gradually eliminated the subjective egoist's attitude. Every time in her Guru Yoga practice, she was able to achieve spiritual response and, whenever she invoked him, she was able to see the Padmakumara appearing to her in great white lights.

This is the boundless and unlimited power of the Buddha Dharma. If not for experiences such as hers, people might not believe it. Mrs. Jung-san Hsueh hopes everyone, including those who are in distress, will sincerely take refuge in the True Buddha School and pay respect to the Holy Red Crown Vajra Master. In this way, they will automatically receive the power from the Master to protect them. Amazing responses will then appear one by one in front of them.

Mrs. Jung-san Hsueh did not have the intention of boasting about her ability in meditation, nor did she want anyone to praise her because of her mystical experiences. But she just couldn't help revealing the facts, and she honestly wanted to let others know that she was grateful to the Bodhisattvas for their protection. At the same time, she wanted to prove that the Holy Red Crown Vajra Master is one of the greatest masters and that he is the same as a Buddha.

The construction of Rey Tseng Temple (Ling Shen Ching Tze) in Redmond, Washington is scheduled to be completed in the middle of 1985. Inside the temple, the main deity will be Kuan Yin Bodhisattva (Avalokitesvara) in the middle, the Golden Mother of the Primordial Pond on the right, and Ksitigarbha on the left. The mystical experiences of Buddhas and Bodhisattvas have increased the confidence of our students. Bodhisattvas are actually "responding to any help anywhere, acting like a boat carrying people across the sea of sufferings."

The Holy Red Crown Vajra Master has made a compassionate vow for the cause of eliminating illusions. He wants all students to cleanse their three negative karmas [of body, speech, and mind], to practice together the Padmakumara Vajra Yoga, and continuously chant the Guru Heart Mantra. If students do this, they will receive mystical experiences, which is one of his wishes.

14. The Manifestation of the Guru's Heart Mantra

Lian-chen of Belgium is a disciple with strong psychic power. He studied with a guru in India for three years and, later in Tibet, he studied with a lama for two years. In Belgium, he heard about the Master and took refuge in the Holy Red Crown Vajra Master.

In Belgium, Lian-chen uses his psychic power to cure illnesses for people. One time, there was a Belgian woman, Debbie, who often had hallucinations due to mental illness.

Lian-chen stretched out his palm before Debbie and chanted the Guru's Heart Mantra, "Om ah hum, guru bei, ah ho sa sa ma ha, Lian-shen siddhi hum." He willed the light energy from his palm into Debbie's mind, while chanting the mantra continuously.

Debbie shouted, "I saw it! I saw it!"

He asked, "What did you see?"

"It is a man sitting on a flower that radiates white light. That flower is very beautiful, a huge flower. It can fly and the man on it can fly too. This is very nice to look at. It is just wonderful! That man is Oriental, wearing a big, beautiful red hat, and a black dress."

"Is there also the color brown on the dress?" asked Lian-chen.

"Yes, two kinds of colors."

"Take a closer look, is there anything else?"

"There is a pearl necklace on his chest."

"That's not a necklace, it's a Buddhist mala for

69

chanting." Lian-chen said.

Lian-chen figured what Debbie saw was the spiritual light of Holy Red Crown Vajra Master. That was the effect of chanting the Guru's Heart Mantra — the light coming instantly from America to Belgium.

This was unimaginable. Although he couldn't see the Master himself, he could feel the energy getting stronger in his palms and going out through his fingers. That had never happened to him before. He was very pleased.

Debbie said, "Oh! That Oriental man reached his hand out and placed it on my head. I feel very nice and comfortable. Everything is beautiful like sun rays coming down into my heart. All the negative things are vanishing. When the sun's rays come, darkness is gone."

Debbie seemed to be becoming normal. According to her family, she had had serious hallucinations and seen things other people couldn't see. Some of the things she saw were dinosaurs, little dwarfs, water creatures in the lake, flower spirits in the forests, and an old, weird man who came to talk to her at night.

The family told Lian-chen that Debbie had never before seen an Oriental man sitting on a big white flower.

Her hallucinations came and went at odd times and she alternated between normal and abnormal reality. Finally, Lian-chen showed my Dharma picture to Debbie, who pointed at it and said, "That's the Oriental man on a big white flower. He placed his hand on my head and treated my illness. That's he for sure."

Lian-chen continued to help Debbie and each time she saw the Master come to her. Her hallucinations gradually disappeared. Everything became normal for her. There were no more dinosaurs, dwarfs, water creatures, flower spirits, or weird old men.... They stopped visiting her.

Debbie's family was very grateful to Lian-chen because she had been very sick and weak for many years

70

from the effects of the hallucinations. In Belgium, she had been to the best psychiatrists, and had stayed in a hospital for therapy. She had even gone to France to have her brain waves checked and had been given a total of approximately one hundred of tranquilizer shots. All efforts were in vain.

Lian-chen told Debbie's family, "Debbie is very lucky because, when I chanted the Guru's Heart Mantra, she saw him. And she was right, it was the Master who cured her illness."

"Who is your Master?"

"He is in America, he is a great Buddhist Master."

"Americans are lucky to have such a great Master living there."

"Yes, he knows the greatest Tantra and wants the people of the world to generate their best Bodhi-mind to practice to become Buddhas. Right now, he is trying to spread the Buddhist teachings. He has a great many of students." Lian-chen gave Debbie and everyone in her family a mala, taught them how to chant the Guru's Heart Mantra, how to take refuge in the Master and helped them to write letters. He told them, "The Holy Red Crown Vajra Master's Heart Mantra is a universal mantra. By reciting it sincerely, you'll receive protection from the Buddhas and Bodhisattvas."

After this incident, Lian-chen was more confident in the Guru's Heart Mantra. It certainly produced amazing responses. He continued to use it to heal many people's mental afflictions. As a result, he is becoming famous in Belgium.

He always told people, "If you want to get rid of your karmic illnesses, you should recite the Guru's Heart Mantra morning and night. If you recite it up to two hundred thousand times, you will have built up a great affinity with the Pure Land of the Buddha kingdom. Whenever you supplicate, do it sincerely, and you'll receive a response. The merits received from reciting the mantra of the Padmakumara can relieve one of sickness and suffering."

Also in Belgium, there was a pregnant woman. Normally she felt the frequent movements of the fetus. Suddenly, there wasn't any movement at all. This lasted for a week, then she panicked and went to the doctor for a check-up. The doctor told her that the baby was dead. She was very grieved and went to see Lian-chen. Lian-chen asked her to recite the Guru's Heart Mantra. When she reached ten thousand recitations, the baby inside her started to move again! She went back to the doctor, who was stupefied and wondered why the baby lived!

The miracles performed by the Holy Red Crown Vajra Master in Belgium were extraordinary responses. People were astonished upon hearing them.

The Master has mentioned before that the number of mental patients the Master has cured could fill up trains full of cars. Here is a sampling of a succession of people: a woman living next to the Taichung Library in Taiwan, a high school principal, a little village girl, a Hong Kong movie star, a Hong Kong singer, a trade merchant, a secondary school teacher, a Catholic nun ...

First, I healed the woman, who introduced me to the high school principal, who, in turn, introduced the little girl and so on. This became a long succession of people coming for healing. There were also numerous other such successions. Now Lian-chen is facing the same situation as the Master. Debbie brought someone else, and so on; this chain will continue, without stopping.

This is truly freeing people from pain and suffering.

15. Light From The Mala

Living in New York is a disciple by the name of Lian-shih (Hung-wei Liao). When he saw a set of five magnificent mandala pictures of Gurus, Personal Deities, Buddhas and Bodhisattvas in a Gelugpa temple, he liked it so much that he acquired five sets (a total of twenty-five pictures) and mailed them to me in Redmond, Washington. The five pictures were: Shakyamuni Buddha, Amitabha Buddha, Four-armed Avalokitesvara (Kuan Yin), Cintamani Avalokitesvara, and Guru Tsongkhapa. They were indeed extraordinary and magnificent.

At this time, another disciple from Chicago, Lianpan (Pao-p'ing Wei) came to see me. Lian-pan was going to set up a Tantric shrine at home, so I gave him one set of the pictures to frame and hang on the wall above his altar, to make it look more magnificent.

At the same time, I also gave him a mala, which I had especially empowered by the following procedure: first I picked up the largest bead with my right hand, then I coiled the mala three times around the four fingers of my left hand, then transferred it to my right hand. To empower it, I formed the Lotus Mudra and raised the mala above my crown, while visualizing my body multiplying into a thousand. I then recited seven times the following mantras:

"Om, namo svaha."

"Om, huai-lu-jia-na mo-la, svaha."

"Om, fa-ji-la gu-ha-ya ga-ba samaya, hum."

After this recitation of the mantras, one round of the

mala (counting the beads for recitation) is equivalent to having one thousand rounds of the mala.

I told Lian-pan if he sincerely recited the Guru's Heart Mantra, then evil would be turned to good fortune and he would be saved in case of danger. This is because the Guru's Heart Mantra is the ultimate, wonderful Dharma of the Great Sun Tathagata (Mahavairocana), and is also the king of all mantras. It is a mantra of great luminosity. With this mantra all evils will be chased away.

Lian-pan took the pictures and the mala back to Chicago. He set up an altar and hung the mala on the wall. He took it down only when he did his practice. Every day he recited the Guru's Heart Mantra one hundred eight times or one thousand eighty times.

One day, Lian-pan's wife, Lian-c'hi, who was also a disciple of the Master, went to pick up their child's birthday cake, which she had ordered earlier from a bakery in Chicago's Chinatown. As she was walking down the street, a speeding car made a left turn and almost ran into her. In order to avoid running over her, the car screeched loudly to a stop. Startled, Lian-chi was shaken and lost her balance. As she fell down, she hit the back of her head on the curb and was knocked unconscious. Luckily, someone at a nearby store recognized her and immediately informed Lian-pan. When Lian-pan arrived, he rushed her to the hospital. By this time, her face and nails had already turned a darkish gray. The doctors tried to resuscitate her.

While the doctors were trying to save her, Lian-pan didn't know what to do. Suddenly, he thought of reciting the Guru's Heart Mantra. He quickly went home and returned with the mala. By this time, his wife's eyes had rolled up, and both her face and nails had turned dark. Shaking their heads, the doctors concluded that she had a brain concussion and that there was little hope.

Holding the mala, Lian-pan calmly and sincerely chanted the Guru's Heart Mantra — praying that the Buddhas, Bodhisattvas and Master would save Lian-chi. When he came to the third round of the mala, the dark color on Lian-chi's face and nails started to recede. Her skin gradually returned to its normal, pinkish color, and she finally woke up and was able to talk.

She told her husband: "I fell and blacked out and knew nothing after that. I didn't even know if I were dead or not. After a while I became aware of something. I saw a circle of very bright white light in front of me. I looked closer and saw it was a mala that emitted light. The mala was circling. The beads and the light made me feel extremely comfortable and relaxed. It was just like going from a place of darkness into a bright world. At the same time, I heard the chanting of the Guru's Heart Mantra and, unconsciously, I joined in and started chanting myself. Then I woke up."

"What did you see?" Lian-pan asked.

"Nothing, except the mala and the light."

"That's it, the Master has especially empowered this mala. Since we have been chanting the Guru's Heart Mantra regularly, when there was danger, this mala and the Guru's Heart Mantra acted as a protecting charm releasing bright light. It saved your life. This mala is really our life saver. It was the grace of the Buddhas, Bodhisattvas and Master. We must thank the Master."

Another instance occurred.

Lian-pan has a younger sister named Hsiao-p'ing Wei, also living in Chicago. She suffered from migraine headache. Once the headache started, she would be in terrible agony and unable to move. Lian-pan felt pity for her and decided to chant the mantra to help her.

One time, when the migraine attacked again, she was

lying on the bed groaning. Lian-pan lit an incense, begging the Master, Buddhas and Bodhisattvas to empower him. He started reciting the Guru's Heart Mantra for about two rounds of the mala. Then, he placed the mala on her head. Miraculously, the pain stopped. Not only that, it never recurred. She had had migraines for more than ten years and they occurred about seven or eight times a month. After her brother's recitation, she was completely back to normal and did not even have to take pain-killers anymore. It was a miracle. Hsiao-p'ing Wei promised her brother that she would come to Redmond to take refuge in the Master.

It had been quite useless to get Hsiao-p'ing Wei to take refuge, because she was a Catholic and had always opposed her brother's belief in Buddhism. But, because of the miracle, she no longer opposed him and she started to believe in the power of Holy Red Crown Vajra Master Lian-shen. She wanted to come to take refuge herself.

The effectiveness of the chanting is not restricted to the Guru's Heart Mantra. One can also recite the name of Amitabha Buddha or Kuan-yin Bodhisattva. Chanting the names of Buddhas and Bodhisattvas has many advantages. It can eliminate negative karmas, enable one to achieve one-point concentration of the mind, and accumulate unimaginable merits. In the Pure Land sect, through chanting the name of Amitabha, a practitioner is able to be reborn in the Western Paradise of Ultimate Bliss, if he or she reaches a continual state of mindfulness of Amitabha.

Chanting the name of Buddha is one of the best ways to liberate oneself from sufferings.

I, the Holy Red Crown Vajra Master Lian-shen, the Tantrika, have spent many years chanting the name of Amitabha, and have attained a great amount of realization from it. Although the current practice is mainly

Tantra, I still have not relinquished chanting the name of Amitabha.

I am a practitioner in Taoism, Sutrayana and Vajrayana Buddhism.

16. Initiation of An Eminent Monk

My student, Lian-kao, was a professor at the National Cheng Chi (Political) University in Taipei. His home was in Kaohsiung and, therefore, during the holidays, he always traveled back and forth between these two cities. One day, just before his bus pulled away, a monk came on board and happened to sit beside Lian-kao. The monk was of medium build and about sixty years old. His round face displayed an achievement of merits. His eyes were full of spirit. Lian-kao guessed that he was not just an ordinary monk.

Lian-kao folded his palms and paid respect to the monk.

The monk said, "Mmm, good." Sitting very peacefully, the monk would sometimes rest with his eyes closed, and sometimes he would count the mala and recite the name of Buddha.

Watching the monk, Lian-kao took out a book, *A Detailed Exposition of Mahamudra*, from his briefcase. He started reading it.

"Oh, you read Sheng-yen Lu's books?" the monk noticed and asked.

"Yes, do you know him?"

"No, but most monks or practitioners know about him and we have even discussed him in our meetings."

"Is there something wrong with Master Sheng-yen Lu?"

"Well ... it's difficult to explain. Anyway, his books

are very controversial and somewhat mysterious and, being a lay Buddhist, he accepts monks as his students! The number of people who slander him is great. It is very hard to distinguish whether he is good or evil. According to hearsay, he changed the name of his sect. He lived in Taiwan before and is now in the United States. He talked about supernatural powers and Buddha Dharma. Sometimes he talked about Taoism, sometimes Buddhism. He said he has already attained the Tao. Therefore, many of my Buddhist fellows consider him a devil cloaked in Zen."

"What is a devil cloaked in Zen?"

"According to my Buddhist fellows, Sheng-yen Lu is a very diligent practitioner in Zen meditation. Most probably he was possessed by devils and therefore has evil powers. All his progress and writings are the effects of devils. They think he doesn't understand and that he assumes he has actually achieved realization. Some Buddhist masters denounce him directly, some just feel pity for him."

"Then, why have so many monks and nuns gone to take refuge in him?"

"Well, ... they are also not perfect ones! You read his books, do you know him?"

"Yes, I do. I got acquainted with him when he was giving a speech in the legislative hall. During that time, Master Lu was quite tearful, giving off a sense of child-like innocence. Later, he cured my brother-in-law's mental illness. I studied his books and felt they were not evil or unorthodox, so I took refuge in him too. My refuge name is Lian-kao."

"Oh!"

"Master Sheng-yen Lu's writings are true and genuinely from the heart. He has studied a lot and fully understands and comprehends Taoism, Sutrayana and Vajrayana Buddhism. There is no doubt about that. He is like a talented man of literature, who can write novels, prose and poems, and is good in all of them. What is wrong with that? Besides, if he is the devil, how can he dissect and analyze the states of Buddha and Mara so thoroughly in his books? How can he specialize in treating patients who are possessed? Many practitioners have said he was the devil, yet they only slandered and criticized him; no one was compassionate enough to "save" him. They just tell others to be compassionate. What is the matter with these people? Today, seventy-thousand[1] students have already taken refuge in him. Are these people all blind, recognizing a devil as their teacher?"

"Well....I have only heard about him from others. I have never read his books. Well, when I have a chance, I will read some of them. How many books has he already published?"

"Fifty-seven books[2]."

"That many! I assume you have already been initiated. What did he teach you?"

"I learned the Pure Land, which is reciting the name of Buddha. When the mind and the Buddha become one, one will be reborn in the Western Paradise and become a Buddha."

"Well, there's nothing wrong with it! There's nothing wrong with it!" The monk kept praising.

During the trip, Lian-kao and the monk happily discussed Buddhist doctrines. When the monk realized Lian-kao was a professor at the National Cheng Chi University, he had even more respect for him. Lian-kao explained to him very clearly the doctrine of the three se-

---

[1] As of 1993, there are over 1,000,000 students all around the world who have taken refuge in Grand Master Lu.

[2] As of 1993, there are over 100 books in Chinese published by Grand Master Lu.

crets. The monk reasoned that the doctrine was correct and it was the right Dharma to purify the body, speech and mind.

Lian-kao gave him three books: *The Highest Yoga Tantra and Mahamudra, A Detailed Exposition of Mahamudra,* and *The Teaching of Dzogchen.*

After the monk returned to his temple, he read all three books. His heart was deeply moved by the books and he felt a kind of ease and comfort in him that he had never felt before. He wondered how could the Master be a devil cloaked in Zen when his books were so well written, clear and easy to understand? The writings indicated a tranquillity achieved when one entered into Samadhi.

This monk, who was a Dharma master, wanted to learn "The Teaching of Dzogchen," so he wrote to me describing how he had come to know about me. I told him to visit me at the Redmond temple the next time he came to the States to spread the Dharma. I would wait for him. Then I would empower him and transmit the teaching to him. (This eminent monk had preached in America before.) I promised to transmit the teaching of Dzogchen to him.

The eminent monk was the chief abbot of three temples. One of his students had a tumor. The monk wanted me to heal him, so I used my *remote psychic healing* method. The tumor of the monk's student turned soft, shrunk in size and began disappearing. This amazed everyone in the temple, but the monk did not reveal that it was Master Sheng-yen Lu who healed the student's tumor.

At the time of this writing, the eminent monk has already taken refuge and received remote empowerment. He holds a notable position in the Buddhist community, and it would be inappropriate for me to disclose his name. In any case, the True Buddha School has gained one more person of great intuition.

The Master has come and taken this incarnation because the time is ripe.

The slander which the Master has to endure is taller than a mountain. A student, Lian-mu, who is a nun, cried as she learned of the slanders suffered by the Master. She had a statue of the Fold-Hand Kuan-yin Bodhisattva sculptured and secretly had it sent to the Master, hoping it would alleviate the Master's sufferings.

In fact, I have no desire for fame. I have reached, through cultivation, a realm where slanders do not bother me.

In the Treatise of the Greater Prajñaparamita Sutra, it says, "The compassion of all Buddhas and Bodhisattvas is indeed great. Compassion is the root of Buddha Dharma. When the Bodhisattvas see sentient beings suffering from the pain of birth, old age, sickness and death, the pain of the body, affliction of the mind, the hardship of this life, and of future life, they will save them with great compassion from these sufferings. The Bodhisattvas should have long gone into nirvana, but have refused to do so. Because of this, compassion is the greatest in Buddhism."

The Master knows only compassion. He does not have such feeling as likes or dislikes, love or hatred.

So all the slanders, abuses, and insults make no difference to me. To someone who has already achieved the state of Emptiness, there is no attachment to fame.

Therefore, Master is one who has "no desire for fame," only compassion.

17. A Wish

Lin Hsiao-jen, one of my students, is a sincere Tantric practitioner. His refuge name is Lian-mo. He has had four gurus: the first was Rinpoche Chiang; the second one was His Holiness, the Sixteenth Gywal Karmapa; the third was Rinpoche Tseng-kang; the last was the Holy Red Crown Vajra Master Lian-shen, the Tantrika.

Lian-mo has also taken refuge in a Sutrayana teacher, Dharma master Chu-yün. In addition, he has taken the Bodhisattva Vows. A great supporter of Buddhism, he has been a vegetarian for many years, recites sutras and practices diligently.

His refuge name "mo" (literally silence) reflects his personality. He is a reticent person, usually reciting the name of Buddha quietly to himself. He works for a large company and is honest with his work. Because of this, he was promoted to a supervisory position. Due to his honest personality and his not knowing how to brag and flatter, he had been stuck in this position for a long time. He was regularly passed over whenever there was an opening for the manager's position.

In June, 1984, the manager's position in the company was vacant again and, according to seniority and work capabilities, Lin Hsiao-jen should have been the pick among the four supervisors who were considered for the position. The other three supervisors had far less experience and were less capable. Everyone started to congratulate him.

However, the newest of the other three supervisors was well-versed in social contacts, young and slick, and had the trust of the director. So rumor spread that this young supervisor had been secretly working to get the new position and the director would most likely favor him.

After hearing the rumor, Lin Hsiao-jen went on quietly chanting the name of Buddha and doing his work. Everyone felt the company was being unfair to him, but they couldn't do anything. When Lin Hsiao-jen went home, he started praying to the Buddha, reciting the Diamond Sutra. He knelt down, bowing until his knees were sore. With tears in his eyes, he recited the names of Buddhas. He was grieved. His colleagues sympathized with him, but it was useless.

Suddenly, he decided to seek help from the Master. But, the Master was in Redmond, Washington, U.S.A. Sending a letter would be too slow and it seemed rude to ask for help over the phone. So he decided to take a four-day holiday, fly to Seattle, and return after one night's stay.

After Lian-mo made the decision, he called Redmond to make an appointment to see the Master. The next day, he requested the four-day leave and bought an airplane ticket.

Without a second thought, he boarded the plane, and flew to Seattle via Tokyo. Because of his eagerness to see the Master, fatigue and arduous travel did not bother him. He thought the Master must have the ability and the way to help him; he had full confidence in the Master.

When the plane was flying above the clouds over the Pacific Ocean, Lian-mo looked ahead and the destination seemed far away. Looking back, the return was also full of uncertainties .... Lian-mo felt a little dizzy and confused in the plane. All he could do now was to continue on to where he originally wanted to go and just tell the Master about his wish. He calmed down but wondered if the

Master would laugh at him and tell him that he was silly. To pull himself together he kept chanting the name of Amitabha Buddha and the Guru's Heart Mantra.

As soon as he saw the Master, he knelt down and sobbed.

"Everything is all right now." I said.

After I brought him to the True Buddha Tantric Quarter, he told me the whole story.

"Do you have to be the manager?" I asked.

"It is a battle I cannot lose!"

Right away, I promised I would help him in this matter and would perform a yoga for him. I put some fresh food into a container and chanted twenty-one times the Food Transformation Mantra: "Namosadpo Dandabiuda Pargeedi Om Sabolasabola Hum." Then I put the container into the Pacific Ocean.

From the sky over the Pacific Ocean, there descended many Celestial Beings to receive the offerings. I told them, "This is the wish of Lian-mo. He hopes to become the manager, please help him."

Chanting the Food Transformation Mantra and forming the corresponding mudra will allow one to obtain amazing help from the Celestial Beings. Because of their receipt of the offerings, the Celestial Beings will help worldly beings to get what they wish.

This is one of the Wonderful Celestial Beings Dharma.

After his one night, Lian-mo went back to Taiwan.

On that same night, the director of Lian-mo's company had a strange dream: sitting on an ocean was a sage, with a gem-umbrella above his head that emitted lights of rainbow colors. The director bowed to this sage, approached and requested guidance. The sage told him that, to get all the benefits he wanted for his company, he should have someone who was obedient and kind to look after his business.

"Where can I find such a person who is obedient and kind?" (Note: Hsiao-jen, Lian-mo's real name, literally means "obedient and kind" in Chinese.)

"Don't you have a person by the name of Lin Hsiao-jen in your company?"

At this point, the director woke up. He felt such a dream was strange and tried to figure out what it meant. It seemed to mean that the sage wanted Lin Hsiao-jen to be the manager, so he told his wife this. His wife replied that Lin Hsiao-jen had worked for many years as a supervisor and should have been the manager long before. Although he was serious in his work and honest, he did not know how to socialize, so the director was not fond of him. But he never made a mistake in his work. He was really the backbone of the company and should be trustworthy enough for this managerial job.

After such a dream and after his wife reminded him, the director started to feel that he had somewhat intentionally passed over Lin in past promotions. He felt a little guilty. So he called Lin Hsiao-jen to his office and told him that he would be the new manager. He also told him about the strange dream he had had. After telling Lin that he should do a good job, he told him that he would announce his promotion in three days.

Lin Hsiao-jen is now the manager.

This true event proves that it is important to honestly believe in the power of the Master and not be suspicious. If one recites the Guru's Heart Mantra, one will be successful in what one sets out to accomplish. This is an incredible, divine mantra!

Lian-mo's trip to Seattle resulted in a miracle.

The response of Bodhisattvas and the help of the Celestial Beings are indeed genuine.

18. The Image In The Sky

A female student, Lian-fei, is from a rich family. Everybody knows that her father is very wealthy. She was a Christian before but, after reading my book, *My Communication with the Spirit World*, took refuge in me and also in the Reverend Master Kuang-ch'in of Tucheng.

Reverend Master Kuang-ch'in taught Lian-fei to chant the Great Compassion Dharani and gave her the refuge-name Ch'uan-ch'üan.

I taught Lian-fei to recite the Guru's Heart Mantra.

She has always been very busy, as she is in charge of some of the enterprises in her father's company. She can only recite the Great Compassion Dharani seven times in the morning and the Guru's Heart Mantra one hundred eight times at night.

One night in February, 1984, she dreamt of the Master, who was standing on a cloud above, talking to her. "The day after tomorrow you are fated to have an accident. Your car will overturn during a long distance trip. But don't be afraid, Padmakumara will protect you. Ill luck will be turned into good and you will escape unharmed."

Right after that she woke up. She wondered why the Master had appeared to her in the dream, and if it were true.

The next night she had the same dream again. She again saw the Master standing above her on a cloud. He repeated to her exactly the same warning, that the next day she would encounter a destined accident, and that

Padmakumara would protect her.

Early in the morning, after she arrived at her company, the business supervisor and the payroll supervisor told her that they all would have to leave the next morning at 7:00 a.m. for a meeting at 1:00 p.m. at the branch in South Taiwan. They would be going in the company's luxurious Lincoln, driven by the company's chauffeur.

She was unwilling to go because of the two dreams, but she couldn't avoid attending the meeting. She was afraid people might laugh at her if she told them about her dreams. Also, she had always been a person of strong will and it was not in her nature to back out. Thinking that the Master would protect her so that the fated accident would not occur, Lian-fei didn't worry anymore and decided to go. After all, it could have been her own imagination that was worrying her.

Early the next morning at 7:00 a.m., the three associates and the chauffeur began the journey, cruising at a high speed. The sky was blue and clear, the highway was flat and smooth, the car was big and spacious. It seemed unlikely that an accident would happen. At about ten o'clock, after they passed through the town of Chiayi, the weather started to cloud over and it began to drizzle continuously. Lian-fei told Old Liu, the chauffeur, not to go too fast. Actually Old Liu was driving at a moderate speed.

Very soon, they exited the highway and turned into the downtown area of Kaohsiung. By then, it was already noon. Lian-fei thought it had been a very smooth journey. How could there be any disaster now? It looked as if her dream of the Master's warning was not at all accurate. It was just herself worrying too much about the dream, which she had thought could be true. She smiled to herself.

While she was pondering the matter, they were cruising on the San To Road. The car in front of them sped up, in an attempt to clear a yellow light, but had to brake hard because the light changed so quickly to red. The Lincoln, which was following closely behind, had to brake hard too. The wheels screeched. Right behind the Lincoln was a big cargo truck which also tried to brake, but failed to come to a complete halt in time. The truck smashed into the back of the Lincoln and shoved it forward, hitting the car in the front. Out of control, the Lincoln rolled over on its right side.

Lian-fei crawled out of the Lincoln and looked up to see the Holy Red Crown Vajra Master's image appearing in the sky standing on a large lotus with golden white petals. He was smiling, wearing a Five Buddhas Crown, a yellow robe and a red cassock. The Master was holding a vajra sceptre in his right hand and a vajra bell in his left hand. His body was emitting wave-like rays of golden white light. He looked magnificently like a Buddha.

Lian-fei immediately knelt down and very humbly bowed to the Master. Then, she went to check the chauffeur and the supervisors. The chauffeur had received cuts and was bleeding from a head injury. The business supervisor had cuts on his arms and the payroll supervisor was unhurt.

An ambulance came and took the injured to the hospital. The payroll supervisor then asked Lian-fei, "Who did you bow to by the road side just now?"

"My Master," Lian-fei replied without hesitation.

"Master, what master?"

"The Holy Red Crown Vajra Master. He is a transformation of Padmakumara. He appeared in the sky as I was crawling out of the car. He smiled to me. Really, it was the Master on top of the clouds in the sky."

"So, your refuge name is Lian ...?"

"Lian-fei. It's the refuge name that Master gave me."

"I am Lian-t'i. I am also a student of the Master. So, the daughter of the chairman of the board is also a student of the Master. I did not know that." The payroll supervisor was clearly surprised.

So, they found out they were fellow practitioners. Lian-fei told Lian-t'i about the dreams she had had, how she was warned by the Master, and how she saw him in the sky right after the accident. Lian-t'i looked up into the sky, but saw nothing. He asked the people around who reacted in a surprised and disbelieving manner, and said they did not see anything.

"Although I did not see the Master, he also protected me. That's why I wasn't hurt either," Lian-t'i said.

"Yes, it was he who saved us," Lian-fei sighed.

I actually considered revealing the real name of Lian-fei. But most of the members of her family are Christians. She is the only one who has taken refuge in the True Buddha School, so she decided not to have her name used in order to avoid stress in the family. Her family does not quite understand the Master yet, and the minister of their church often attacks the Master during his sermons.

The other person involved in the accident, Lian-t'i, works at the company, so I cannot reveal his real name either. Lian-t'i always advises others to sincerely recite the Guru Heart Mantra of the *Namo Great Compassionate Lian-shen Bodhisattva-Mahasattva,* as it can indeed relieve sufferings and ease difficulties.

So, the image of the Master in the sky was, indeed, real.

That was the manifestation of one of the billion transformations of Padmakumara, emitting thousands and millions of rays in wonderful light waves.

19. The Cause of Faith in Buddhism

On March 19, 1985, I received an invitation from Kushi-nagara, India to attend the celebration in remembrance of the birth of Shakyamuni Buddha 2,550 years ago. It was an invitation especially for masters of great achievement.

As far as I know, although Buddhism no longer pre-vails in India (the Indians are mostly believers in Hin-duism), there are still two important Buddhist sacred places. One is Sarnath, where the Buddha gave his first sermon on the Eight-Fold Paths, and the other is Kushi-nagara, where the Buddha entered into nirvana.

It is said that only the highly knowledgeable ones and masters of great accomplishments were invited. All preparations for the ceremony were underway.

The first sacred place, Sarnath, is the famous Mrga-dava (Deer Park). It was there that the Buddha gave his first discourse after his awakening to the five Bhik-shus. The site has been reconstructed on fifteen acres of land. There are deer wandering about and there are lotus ponds.

The second sacred place has a huge statue of a sleep-ing Buddha.

How did I get such a grand invitation? The reason was an East Indian Tantric practitioner, Dr. Harkrvshna, who had come to see me in Seattle. He was a member of the Great Bodhi Society in India and was one of those in-volved in organizing the celebrations. He understood that Master Sheng-yen Lu of the United States was someone who had attained great realization, and so invited me.

During the ceremony, an honor certificate would be given out by the Governor of Sikkam. The Holy Red Crown Vajra Master would be one of the masters to be awarded the certificate. On the certificate it says "The Master has great perception and knowledge, possesses complete understanding of the Buddha's teachings, has disciples throughout the world, and is recognized by Buddhist scholars worldwide. The following honor goes to the Master: Carry forward the priceless teachings of the Buddha. Preserve the Truth and the Valued, Develop the Truth and the Valued."

It was a great honor for me.

Students and readers will understand that all the great efforts of the Master's are gaining recognition in the world.

A sage once said: "When the righteous paths decline and the evil practices are all over the world, there will appear a true master."

And now, light has gradually appeared and darkness has begun to fade away. In fear, evil attacks *Him*. But, He and the universe are one. When man attacks the Universe, will the Universe suffer any loss?

Many students, many tens of thousands will, in due course, take faith in Buddhism because of Holy Red Crown Vajra Master.

Here are some excerpts from letters written by students about their feelings:

"Relying on the living Bodhisattva, I feel myself full of Dharma joy. It's hard to express how great the Master is. With the attainment of realization, the Master has become the everlasting and boundless Dharma Body which we forever seek.

"I know the only way to find the truth is to follow

a real Master. The universe and Master are one and, therefore, the Master is our source of learning.

"It was really unimaginable. I have never experienced things like this before. I saw strong white light surging from the Master's forehead into my brow point. Everytime, when I think of the Master's white light of blessing, I felt the greatness of the Master. It makes me feel like crying."

— Lian-t'i, Indonesia

"Master Lu has already given me a lot. We are very fortunate to be students of the Master. My thirty-odd years of migraine headache were completely cured by merely taking refuge by remote empowerment. I didn't see the doctor nor did I take any medicine. It was just completely cured the day after the empowerment. This wasn't a coincidence!

"The power of the Master is far beyond the level of our comprehension. This is an invisible power. Students can experience it no matter what country they reside in. Master is like the sun and the moon shining on all of us.

"After reading *The Teachings of Dzogchen*[1], I realize how pure, how holy the Master is. I sigh with feeling that the thoughts of worldly people are imperfect and insincere.

"Three bows to the Master. Namo guru bei — our forever great Master."

— Lian-yu, Republic of China

"I felt time flying when I was with the Master and never found it was enough. It is hard to describe my happiness when I saw the Master during a blessing ceremony in 1985. I saw the sunlight and the moonlight auras around the Master, radiating out like thousands of light

---

[1] The 56th book of Grand Master Lu, published in 1985.

rays. Even when I closed my eyes, the lights were still shimmering. I know I have never experienced anything like this and I will never forget it. One cannot comprehend this kind of feeling without actually experiencing it.

"I remember with gratitude that the Master taught us, in detail, about meditation and the practice of the three great mystical Dharmas, and led us to progress along the path of Tantric practices.

"In the ceremony, I saw many Westerners bowing to the Master, receiving the "Divine (Triple Hum) Water" empowerments. Living beings of the world are receiving the generosity of the Master. This kind of salvation and the pure, divine water really cleanse worldly beings of their impurities. I believe firmly that Master is the transformation of the ancient Buddha. I really saw it and recognized it. I also have attained a certain level of achievement.

"Returning to my country, I, too, should spread the Master's teachings."

— Lian-lu, Canada

Many students have already tasted the joy of the Dharma. This global brightness has only just started to radiate. It is the result of the unimaginable merits of the Master, eradicating the worries of those who encounter it. To get away from suffering, people should take refuge and learn the teachings.

Mystical experiences are irrefutable facts. If people humbly seek verification, they will get close to the Truth. Compassion is the virtuous characteristic of the Holy Red Crown Vajra Master. Let's all chant: "Om ah hum, guru bei, ah-ho-sa-sa-ma-ha, Lian-shen siddhi hum" and head toward the Lian-shen Buddha land.

20. The Mystical Experiences of a Ph.D.

On the night of March 20, 1985 at eight o'clock in the evening, two cars arrived at my residence. One belonged to Dr. Luo Cheng-fang, from Oregon, the other belonged to Dr. Tseng Wen-ch'in, from Seattle, a well known general practitioner.

Dr. Luo Cheng-fang, who holds a doctorate in forestry and chemistry, brought several boxes of bowls and plates as presents to the Ling Shen Ching Tze Temple, which is scheduled to be inaugurated soon. After the opening of the Temple, visitors will come and meals will be served.

Dr. Tseng Wen-ch'in, of Seattle, was extremely touched by my books. He will be taking refuge in the True Buddha School and promised to be the school's medical consultant. He would like to be the family doctor for all True Buddha disciples and is willing to provide the best medical services, including diagnosis, day and night service, the answering of medical questions, treating physiological problems, etc.. Doctor Tseng's intention to take refuge in the Holy Red Crown Vajra Master Sheng-yen Lu was very sincere.

Besides these two visitors, there were also present the three brothers of the Chen family and Mr. Hung T'ing Mao. So, we all sat around the table talking.

Dr. Luo Cheng-fang's refuge-name is Lian-chih. He received the initiation empowerment on February 19th, 1984. After he went home, he set up his altar and started

95

his practices. He received substantial psychic responses. Now his three channels are completely open.

Dr. Luo said, "Due to a mistake, I didn't receive any notice of the July, 1984, Deliverance Ceremony, so I knew nothing about it. During that time, quite unexpectedly, all my deceased ancestors came visiting, one after another. My grandparents and parents also came, and so did my uncles. Their sudden visits were a mystery."

Dr. Luo continued, "Since my communication with spirits was not quite perfected, I felt that these deceased ancestors were pressing on me, but I didn't understand why. They were very anxious and I was ignorant of their intentions. I really didn't know what to do."

Dr. Luo learned that every year, on the last Saturday in the seventh Lunar month, there is a Bardo Deliverance Ceremony held by the True Buddha School. Unfortunately the ceremony was over by the time he found out about it. Dr. Luo said, "Now, I realize they came for the Bardo Deliverance Ceremony."

Dr. Luo's recent practices involved the use of thought power to invoke his ancestors to line up in front of the Buddha. Then, he visualized them doing the practice together with him and, afterwards, he dedicated the merits to them.

Dr. Luo felt his ancestors were extremely happy. The spirits of the ancestors received the joy of deep meditation and also the taste of Dharma from Buddhas and Bodhisattvas. Only someone with real spiritual contact would totally understand this kind of experience.

Dr. Luo said, "Only one ancestor did not come. He was no longer in the spirit realm, so I couldn't invoke him. I knew about this because the other ancestors told me so."

Dr. Luo has a relative who is a Zen practitioner. He did not understand the power of Tantric practice but, whenever he meditated at Dr. Luo's altar, he always felt the presence of a strong and incredibly concentrated spiritual energy. In temples or any other place where he meditated, he felt nothing like that.

Dr. Luo has started to teach the Buddha Dharma in Portland, Oregon, and possibly will set up a local chapter. He will be receiving the vajra teachings from the Holy Red Crown Vajra Master and, in the future, become an acharya of the True Buddha School.

After listening to Dr. Luo, Dr. Tseng Wen-ch'in mentioned that the American medical community had already started research on the existence of consciousness after death. Some members have also started to examine the questions of "resurrection" and "eternity."

Dr. Tseng said, "Life is short; the average life span of an American is about seventy six years, therefore, reaching out to eternity is most meaningful in life. In this respect, we must try to achieve realization. Life, like that of the Holy Red Crown Vajra Master's, is the most meaningful. Prestige and status are merely temporary."

The evening's conversation was very memorable.

21. The Ancient Jade Bangles

In Jarkarta, the capital city of Indonesia, there is a student whose refuge name is Lian-k'ui. She is a lay Buddhist, about sixty years old, and quite well off. She keeps a pair of ancient jade bangles passed down by her family.

This pair of jade bangles had twice been buried in and disinterred from the earth. This is what happened: the bangles were buried with the ancestors but, later, when the descendants reburied the ancestors' bones, the bangles, were recovered. This happened twice.

From what people say, members of Lian-k'ui's family treat the jade bangles as the family's most treasured heirlooms. The bangles are emerald in color and marked with five-colored clouds. They are in absolutely flawless condition. It is said that, when they are being worn, the person wearing them feels an extremely comfortable and cooling sensation. The colored clouds are also known as blood specks. The jade had been in contact with human blood for a long enough time that it permeated into them, making them spiritually efficacious.

The ancient jade bangles had once been worn by someone who spent a night in a haunted house. Legend has it that the jade emitted an immense green light that prevented the ghosts from entering the house. This amazed a lot of people.

The ancient jade bangles have always been kept in a safe place and were seldom worn by the elderly woman. One day, just after the sun had set and the weather had turned cooler, a couple, who were distant relatives, came with their child from a nearby town to see her. Lian-k'ui happily greeted them. The couple, who had heard of the ancient jade bangles, wished to see them. Without hesitation, Lian-k'ui went into her room and took out the bangles, which were wrapped in a red cloth.

Coincidentally, right after the sun set, the sky became cloudy and it started raining. Seeing this, the old woman hurriedly went out to gather her clothes. The couple followed immediately to help.

When they all returned to the house, they discovered that a strange thing had happened. The ancient jade bangles and the red cloth had disappeared from the table!

Lian-k'ui's face turned pale, and the couple were anxious too. They asked their four year old boy what had happened. He looked blank, panicked when his parents shook him, and began to cry. Lian-k'ui couldn't believe she could lose the bangles in such a short time. Panic-stricken, they searched all around the table and everywhere else in the living room. They could not find them.

Lian-k'ui, feeling dizzy and anxious, didn't know what to do.

She worried that she was old and forgetful and perhaps had never removed the jade bangles after all. So, she went back to her room and checked, but the bangles were not there.

There was no one else in the house beyond the four of them, including the child who was only four years old. Who, then, was the thief? She wondered. Perhaps her relatives had only pretended to come just to see the bangles and had taken them when they had the chance.

But this was impossible. They were Buddhists and looked very honest. There was no reason to suspect them. Yet, after searching the living room thoroughly, there was no trace of the ancient jade bangles.

The couple were in a difficult position as they felt

they were the cause for the disappearance of the valuables. For a long time they tried to help find the bangles, but they searched in vain. Although Lian-k'ui did not suspect them, they did not know what to say. The loss of the bangles was unthinkable and the couple was at a loss what to do. Finally, to show they were innocent, they opened the wife's hand bag and dug out their pockets. They even offered to compensate for the loss of the jade bangles.

Lian-k'ui turned them down immediately, since the bangles were heirlooms and priceless and could not be replaced.

Embarrassed, the couple and the child said goodbye and left.

Lian-k'ui pondered the bangles' disappearance as she sat on a bamboo chair in the dark. She wondered what had happened. She thought of Kuan-yin Bodhisattva, and started chanting, "The compassionate Kuan-yin Bodhisattva, the compassionate Kuan-yin Bodhisattva, I've lost my jade bangles, please, Kuan-yin Bodhisattva, help me to find them."

She also lit incense and bowed to the Master's Dharma picture on the altar. She sincerely prayed to the Master, "Vajra Master Sheng-yen Lu, the transformation of Padmakumara, please guide me with your spiritual light to find the lost jade bangles. They are the family's treasured heirlooms. They can't be lost! Please, the transformation body of Padmakumara, Vajra Master Sheng-yen Lu, help me to get them back with your power," she begged in tears.

She couldn't sleep, tossing and turning most of the night. Sleep only came when it was almost morning. Once she fell asleep, however, she saw Master Sheng-yen Lu sitting on a lotus above an auspicious five-colored cloud. The Master was wearing casual clothing. There was no Five Buddha crown on his head, but he was holding a mala and was reciting the name of Amitabha.

Lian-k'ui shouted, "Master, Amitabha, the jade bangles!"

She saw the Master pointing his finger toward the sky. A shoe appeared. Very soon, the Master and the shoe vanished. Then Lian-k'ui woke up.

Thinking of the shoe pointed at by the Master, she searched all the shoes in the house but could find nothing. She was very disappointed, wondering if it was a mistake that the Master pointed to a shoe.

Lian-k'ui went outside where there was a small vegetable garden. Between the door and the garden she saw a pair of worn-out rain boots. A sudden thought came to her and she quickly reached for the boots. She tried the first boot — there was nothing inside. When she put her hand in the second one she felt something solid, wrapped in cloth. She took it out. It was her ancient jade bangles!

She was shocked and immediately thanked the Bodhisattvas and the Master. She was extremely happy.

According to reconstruction in her letter to me, when she and the couple went out in the rain to gather the clothes, the four-year old boy probably took the bangles in the red cloth and stood by the door, watching them. The boy probably dropped the cloth bundle into the old boot without realizing what he had done.

Anyway, she was grateful to have the bangles back.

22. A Taste of Suffering in Dreams

On the 11th of February, 1984, in Tukwila, Washington, U.S.A., a Blessing Ceremony was held. A week before the Ceremony, the Holy Red Crown Vajra Master suddenly came down with uncontrollable intestinal hemorrhaging. His nose also started to bleed. This continued for seven days.

But, on the day of the Blessing Ceremony, everything was back to normal. The bleeding stopped completely.

The Buddhas and Bodhisattvas indicated that, "The negative karmas of the sentient beings do not disappear unless they are being substituted or transferred to somewhere else."

I finally understood that the bleedings were meant to substitute for the sufferings of the registered participants, because many of them would have to face bleeding episodes, such as car accidents, acute illnesses, or emergency operations. To pray for their blessings, the Master had to supersede. The bleedings, which had been going on for seven days, were to substitute for their bleeding mishaps. This was great evidence of the power of the Blessing Ceremony.

Here lies the great meaning of the Blessing Ceremony!

Ever since I received the Tantra teachings from Padmasambhava, practiced the Highest Tantra Yoga, Maha Mudra, and the Dzogchen, and attained complete realization in all of them, my body has become extremely healthy. I have not had any illnesses at all, not even a cold, fever, sneeze, cough, headache or fatigue. I have become insulated from illnesses.

Many people have the habit of dozing off and taking an afternoon nap. This idea is alien to me. I only sleep when it's time to do so at night. I do not know what fatigue is.

The Holy Red Crown Vajra Master meditates twice daily, entering into the great Vajra Samadhi of Cosmic Consciousness, merging with the Light of the Ocean of Consciousness of Vairocana, and becoming one with the Buddha. The Buddha is the Master and the Master is the Buddha.

Every day, I practice diligently on the *moving meditation*: the Maha Mudra, the seven **chakra** exercises, martial arts, and yoga breathing exercises that enables the energy in the meridians to flow smoothly.

It's the combined every day practice of *sitting meditation* and *moving meditation* that keeps me healthy. Harboring no anger, not losing any seminal energy, possessing a high resistance to illness — these are the reasons attributed by outsiders to the Master's good health.

On March 2nd, 1985, there was another Blessing Ceremony.

Strangely, this time the Master did not experience any further hemorrhaging of the intestine or nose. Neither was there any pain, nor discomfort. Wasn't the Master going to supersede any more? Negative karmas have to be taken by someone else or transferred; they cannot disappear by themselves.

Let me honestly tell my students: the Master had not stopped superseding. He had just superseded in his dreams.

To make this clearer: for a whole week before the ceremony, I had weird dreams every single night. Some examples:

— As I was walking down a street, a car suddenly hit me from behind, running over me, and splattering flesh, blood, and brain matter everywhere.

— In an operating room my body was being cut open and the doctors took out a lot of things and sutured back a lot of other things. I bled profusely and received blood transfusions.

— In an emergency room, I was seriously ill with chronic, acute, and terminal illnesses, such as: fever, cold, arthritis, malaria, diseases of the eyes, nose, tongue, mouth, gums, lips, throat, face, head, neck, chest, ribs, abdomen, hands, back, kidneys, navel, thigh, knees, and feet; I suffered hemorrhoids, diarrhea, phlegm, asthma, leprosy, boils, tumors, herpes, eczema, psychosis, epilepsy, diabetes, uremia, heart disease, pains, and aches, and semi-paralysis, as well as all kinds of nameless demonic illnesses.

— I was alive, then dead; alive, then dead again. One moment I lived, another moment I died. I suffered both the pain of living and dying.

— During this one week the Master tasted all kinds of sufferings in his dreams.

— In one dream, I even hung myself with a rope, suffocating and bleeding around the neck, and my consciousness drifted away from the body.

During the seven days prior to the ceremony, the Master's spirit was unable to control itself. Every night I suffered for the students in all kinds of predicaments in my dreams. This "sufferings in dreams" was inexpressible to others. How could anyone know that during those seven days, the Master had suffered through the worst kinds of torture?

I did not talk about my dream sufferings when they happened. In any case, when I woke up, my body was still healthy and sound, everything was peaceful, my face shone with radiance, and I felt no pain. One rarely hears of this "superseding negative karma in dreams," which is the testimony of authentic Dharma.

From this chapter, it can be seen that students who take refuge in a master of extraordinary lineage will have great advantages. A master of supreme lineage is a realized master, who has the ability to supersede and transfer his students' negative karmas, helping them to learn the highest, Tantric yoga and achieve spiritual accomplishments.

The Tantric yogas taught by the Holy Red Crown Vajra Master are authentic Dharmas; therefore, all his students are learning the authentic Dharmas. Having the authentic Dharmas taught by an authentic master of correct lineage, the students have many mystical experiences — these serve as evidence of the authenticity of the Dharmas.

"Sufferings in dreams" proves that the Master is a complete vajra-master, who has learned the Highest Tantric yogas and can supersede for the negative karmas of all beings, enabling them to attain Buddhahood.

I hope people who want to become Buddhas will exercise caution in their selection of a master. Many people take refuge in the wrong masters (false masters) by mistake, thus destroying their chance of obtaining wisdom. People who want to become Buddhas should take refuge in the real and meritorious Holy Red Crown Vajra Master.

23. The Initiation of a Student of Master Kung

I have a student whose refuge name is Lian-ch'ien. He is an old Tantric practitioner. At the time of this writing, he was preaching in Southeast Asia. Lian-ch'ien is a student of the Kagyupas and Nyingmapas lineage. In 1947, he took refuge in Tulku Kung-ke (1893–1957) at the Nora Pagoda Temple at Lake Hsüan Wu in Nanking.

Tulku Kung-ke, when he was alive, had been honored with the title "The Guidance Counselor, the Broad Enlightenment Zen Master." He passed away on January 29th, 1957. Before 1949 the Chinese Government honored Master Kung with the following designation: *Tulku Kung-ke, a constant exponent of Buddhist teachings, who perpetuates the Sect's practices, and transcribes and propagates Buddhist literature that attract multitudes of believers. In 1937, when the Sino-Japanese War began, Tulku Kung-ke traveled to Kiangsi and Szuchuan Provinces to organize group practices to pray sincerely for the peace of the country. This is worthy of praise. Thus the honor of the title "The Guidance Counselor, the Broad Enlightenment Zen Master" for his distinguished excellence.*

Lian-ch'ien studied with Master Kung for five years, concentrating on the practice of the Blackrobe Vajra Yoga, the Paramasukha-Chakrasamvara Yoga, the Amitabha Yoga, as well as the Great Fire Offering. Lian-ch'ien also took refuge in Master Hua-tzang for a period of time. Around 1961, after the empowerment of Master Hua-tzang, Lian-ch'ien became an acharya. Since then, he has been preaching everywhere. According to my knowledge, Lian-ch'ien first took refuge in Master Kung of the Kagyu lineage, then Master Hua-tzang of the Nyingma lineage and, finally, he took refuge in the True Buddha School, thus obtaining the True Buddha lineage.

Already being an acharya under Master Hua-tzang, he will naturally be, in the future, an acharya of the True Buddha School.

Here is how Lian-ch'ien came to take refuge in me:

While he was in Southeast Asia preaching the Dharma, he heard of Master Sheng-yen Lu.

When he saw the Dharma picture of Master Lu wearing the Five Buddha crown, he said, "That's really sickening."

When he gave teachings, he would cross his legs and close his eyes and say, "Anyone here who is a student of the so called True Buddha School or the so called Master Sheng-yen Lu, please get out of here. I don't teach the evil and the unorthodox."

He asked one of the students, "What kind of lineage is Sheng-yen Lu? How dare he make himself the founder of a sect? When I learned Tantra, he was still a baby! There are so many great sages around, yet no one would dare presume to create a sect. He is just too arrogant and wild."

One time, Lian-ch'ien accepted a student who could be said to have an impeccable moral character, as well as a high level of scholastic achievement in both worldly and Buddhist knowledge. This student told the old practitioner how he had become a Buddhist and also demonstrated to him his Tantric practices. The old man was greatly astonished.

107

He asked, "Whom did you take refuge in? From whom did you learn this?"

"Master Sheng-yen Lu. I learned from him."

The old man did not make a sound; he was completely silent. Finally, he said, "This is simply incredible. Why did you take refuge in Sheng-yen Lu?"

"Because I think his school emphasizes the actual practice of Tantra. The students commit themselves totally to actual practice. Many people have achievements because Master Lu is patient in his teachings. The way I see it, this school is going to continue to flourish in the future. The supernatural power displayed by the Master is an effective way to get the public to learn the teachings. Right from the beginning, when he was learning the Tantra, Master Lu had been considerably slandered by many and had suffered much hardship and affliction. But, the Master has remained unruffled. When I first practiced the Guru Yoga, I immediately received responses. Many people know that Master can subjugate evils, has the divine power to cure illnesses and is efficacious in his divinations. The mystical experiences are just too many to enumerate."

"Is everything that he wrote true?" asked Lian-ch'ien.

"Among my friends, some have actually been cured or rescued. This is true. Word spread from one to thousands, so the number of initiated became many. A friend of mine went into a coma for many days, because of bleeding in his brain. The doctors had given up on him. His family begged Master Lu. My friend actually woke up and began getting better and better each day. It was indeed miraculous."

"Could that be a coincidence?"

"No, it was not a coincidence because it was not the

only incident. Mr. Ch'in-ching Lin who had remained in a psychiatric hospital for five years got well three days after he had taken three charms empowered by the Master."

"Are the contents of Sheng-yen Lu's books true accounts?"

"Would a swindler work so hard, writing fifty seven books, to cheat people? Someone said, even if he were a swindler, his spirit and hard work in writing and studying the Buddha Dharma command our respect. It's still worthwhile to take refuge in him. We would have no regrets — even if he were a swindler."

"Oh, well... well...," Lian-chi'ien continued. "Could he be then the demon in disguise?"

"Demon? Demons are destructive. Are there demons who specialize in helping people? If he is a demon who delivers people, then he is equal to a Buddha who is compassionate to mankind."

On the night of March 17th, 1984, Lian-ch'ien, the old master, was in Thailand. He had a car accident on the road to Pattaya. The other car involved in the head-on collision was a U.S. military truck, driven by a sergeant who had a bar girl with him. The elderly master, whose head crashed into the windshield, lapsed into unconsciousness.

He was taken to the Universal Compassion Hospital.

He could not move at all. While he was unconscious, he saw a Light by the head of his bed and in the center of the Light was someone who looked kind and magnificent. It was Master Sheng-yen Lu.

"Master, is there hope?" Lian-ch'ien asked.

"Don't worry, you'll be saved," the Master said, smiling.

Master Lu pressed both his hands on Lian-ch'ien's head and blessed him.

109

At that moment Lian-ch'ien asked, "I used to condemn you, Master, don't you mind?"

Master smiled and said, "Because you have condemned me, I have come to save you."

"I vow to the Master, if I recover I will become a student of the True Buddha School. I'll not change my mind. I beg Master to empower me."

The third morning, which was the morning of March 20th, Lian-ch'ien woke up. He found he could get up and walk with ease. He remembered very clearly that it was Master Sheng-yen Lu who had saved him. He felt calm, knowing that it was impossible to express in words his admiration for Master Lu, who deserved worship and praise.

Many other Dharma teachers did not understand why this old master had come to take refuge in the True Buddha School.

But Lian-ch'ien said, "This is karma. I have condemned the Master, now I take refuge in him. This is quite unusual but it is true. It has turned me around; it is incredible."

Because of his taking refuge in the True Buddha School, Lian-ch'ien has been condemned by many of his Buddhist fellows, but he feels calm and at ease with himself.

24. A Woman From Alaska

From the icy land of Alaska, an American woman, Melanie, came to Seattle to see a Chinese herbal doctor, Dr. Liao. Dr. Liao had been a Buddhist monk before he resumed household life and pursued a study in Chinese herbal medicine. At present, he runs a clinic in Seattle's Chinatown.

Melanie had seen many western doctors, but they couldn't diagnose the reason for her infertility. Finally, she heard of Dr. Liao and came to see him.

After an examination, which included an analysis of the patient's complexion and pulse, Dr. Liao couldn't find anything physically wrong either. He thought there was something strange about this.

"You should go to see Master Sheng-yen Lu!" said Dr. Liao.

"Who is Master Sheng-yen Lu? What can he do?" Melanie asked.

"Your case is very special. It could be an illness of karma, a case of negative karma. I cannot help you here. I'll give you a phone number. It's Dr. Lu-sheng Chung's number. He is a student of Master Sheng-yen Lu. You can ask him to take you to see Master Lu. Master Lu will know the reason for your problem."

So, Dr. Chung brought Melanie to see me. Once I saw her, I knew the problem.

I held a vajra bell over her head and rang it three times. Melanie was puzzled.

Dr. Chung asked me, "What's the matter?"

I explained that Melanie had been pregnant three times before and had aborted the fetuses. The souls of these three fetuses had not left the body of the mother and had prevented other souls from entering the womb, thereby preventing further pregnancy. Due to their presence in the mother's body, Melanie also suffered from insomnia, unrest, fatigue, and strange dreams.

Indeed Melanie admitted she had all these problems. She also admitted that she had had the three abortions. In America, abortion during the first trimester is legal and the practice of abortion is very common. Unmarried young girls have few alternatives other than abortions. So, in the States, clinics that specialize in abortions usually have a thriving practice.

One should know that the souls of the three fetuses were *water baby spirits.* The three rings of the vajra bell were to draw them out. When the Master was ringing the bell, he was actually applying the Mahamudra Yoga and entering into the Samadhi of the True Void. Though his appearance was normal, the Master was actually concentrating his mind and accomplishing the yoga of summons.

I could detect three rays of pale red light on Melanie. This was the light of the Hungry Ghosts Realm, one of the Six Realms (the lights of the Six Realms are as follows: Heaven — white; Asura — pale green; Human — pale yellow; Animal — pale blue; Hungry Ghost — pale red; Hell — black). So, from my forehead, I emitted a strong red light, which was not to chase away the three pale red lights, but rather to summon them to come to me.

I prayed for the three Water Baby Spirits, "Why are you baby spirits wandering alone, away from all your friends and relatives? In this Universe there are other better and more beautiful places to stay. Do not dwell too long in the body of a mother in the Human Realm!"

I prayed, "All Buddhas and Bodhisattvas, please emit

the great red light of compassion and drive away the fear of these three water baby spirits. Let all negative karmas retreat. The power of Holy Red Crown Vajra Master will eliminate all suffering."

At this time, from the Universe itself, the power of compassion came swirling down and the pure red light led away the three water baby spirits.

The Holy Red Crown Vajra Master is a great compassionate sage. His help for Melanie needed no return. The Master has always quietly and incessantly been doing the work of salvation. The pure light of salvation emitted by the Master is the Light of Samadhi from the Maha Twin Lotus Ponds. This is truly wondrous.

It is important to know that the Light of Samadhi is generated from the turning of the Guru's Heart Mantra Wheel in the true Emptiness. If one's mind is not at peace, but racing with confusing thoughts, there will never be moments of quietness. According to the fixed karmas on such a person, there will be weak lights of the Six Realms appearing. If a Tantric practitioner who has taken refuge in the Master, recites the Guru's Heart Mantra every day, the Samadhi Light of the practitioner will become brighter and brighter, until it finally shines before the practitioner. Then he will be reborn in the Maha Twin Lotus Ponds. This is the result of one-pointed concentration of mind.

The three water baby spirits, attracted by the pure red light, were led by the Most Supreme and returned to the Empty Space.

Thus Melanie's body became purified.

On March 22nd, 1985, Dr. Chung again met Melanie. And this time she was very pregnant.

She was very grateful for his guidance.

But Dr. Chung wanted her to thank Master Sheng-yen Lu and invited her to join us in our group practice.

He wanted her to take refuge in the Master. She decided to take refuge as soon as possible and planned to move from Alaska to Seattle.

On March 23rd, 1985, during our regular Saturday group practice, Dr. Chung talked to the group about his experience and his involvement in this incident, which truly exemplifies the power of Vajra Master Sheng-yen Lu.

The incident reminds me that the Buddha Dharma is going to propagate in the world, especially the West. The Buddha Dharma is going to erect, in Seattle, a great world Dharma Banner. I could see that in the future, Seattle, like Tibet, would be a Buddhist teaching center.

The True Buddha School is now established and it is going to flourish. In the future, I am going to establish the order of practices, such as the Three Studies (discipline, meditation, wisdom), the Three Levels (of Teachings), the Six Perfections, Four Virtues, and techniques of Visualization, etc. I hope more people will benefit from this and achieve realization.

With great compassion, determination and wisdom, the Padmakumara salvages sentient beings of all nationalities. His methods of salvation are sometimes announced, but he also performs many silent miracles. When there is need, there is help. This help is given completely, with delight and without hesitation.

One after one, miracles happen. Can one guess how many more miracles have occurred silently? People should recognize this and generate their Bodhicitta to take refuge in the True Buddha School.

25. The Cement Master

There is a student with the refuge name Lian-tsao. He is a poor cement worker who usually works as a bricklayer. Around the time of the Mid-Autumn Festival in 1984, while he was working for someone building a house, an idea suddenly came to him. He thought of borrowing the new porcelain statue of the Master from a friend. From the statue he could make a mold using sand and mud. Then, he could pour cement into the mold and let it solidify, and he would have a statue of the Master for himself.

He thought of doing this because he was poor. The money he earned was just enough to support his elderly parents, a handicapped sister, and his own family.

Lian-tsao was not successful the first several attempts in making the statue. However, he finally made it and it turned out rather well. After polishing the statue, he added colors, making it look magnificent.

Lian-tsao told the Master that the most difficult part of making the statue was making the Master's hand-held implements, which had to be done separately and then joined to the statue. Apart from that, the statue was exactly the same as the original one. Lian-tsao was very happy and placed it in one corner of his bedroom, covering it with a piece of yellow cloth at night when he went to sleep. Both in the morning and at night, he would light an incense before the statue, then perform prostrations and recite the Guru's Heart Mantra.

Lian-tsao is an honest person. The Master taught

him to chant the name of Amitabha each time he laid a brick. So, he always chanted the name of Amitabha. This came to the knowledge of the contractor and his co-workers who frequently teased him with "Amitabha, eats pork, not carrots." Lian-tsao did not mind; he only smiled and kept on chanting.

One day, some of the cement workers were trying to organize a gang in an attempt to carry out some gambling frauds. One of the leaders tried to coerce Lian-tsao to join, threatening to harm him if he refused. This fellow had in the past frequently harassed Lian-tsao, either hitting him or forcing him to lend him money, which he never paid back.

Lian-tsao was very frightened and extremely worried. When he got home that night, he lit an incense and started bowing before the Master, invoking Padmakumara for help and protection. He cried as he begged and chanted the Guru Heart Mantra, confident that the Master could get him out of this difficulty.

Nevertheless, that gang leader did not let him go, but gathered the gang, armed with weapons, and surrounded Lian-tsao's residence. He forced Lian-tsao to come out to negotiate. Lian-tsao was then seized by his arms on both sides and taken to the woods, where he was beaten with a whip by the leader. Strangely, Lian-tsao did not feel any pain at all when the whip landed on him. Another fellow hit him on the neck with a rod. The rod broke, but Lian-tsao still did not feel any pain.

Luckily, some neighbors had seen him being taken away and informed the police. At the critical moment, the police arrived on the scene, causing the gang to disperse haphazardly.

When Lian-tsao returned home, he lit an incense and bowed to the Master. He was taken aback — some of the colors on the chest and back of the statue had fallen off. There were stripes on the statue, as if it had been whipped. Even stranger, there was a hole in the neck which corresponded exactly with the spot where he had been hit by the rod.

Lian-tsao recalled the moment in which he was beaten — he had felt nothing and his body was completely unhurt. Instead, the statue of the master had stripes on the body and a hole in the neck. He realized that the Master must have been superseding in his place. Extremely touched, he quickly bowed and recited in earnest the Guru Heart Mantra.

Later Lian-tsao added some more colors to the statue and mended the hole in the neck. His confidence in the Master grew even more.

The gang and its leader were summoned by the police and ordered to disband. After this, it was peaceful and quiet. The leader even became remorseful.

When she was alive, the grandmother of Lian-tsao was a Buddhist. She could not read but had the Universal Gateway Article of the Lotus Sutra committed to memory. She was very fond of Lian-tsao.

One night, the grandmother, who had passed away, came to talk to him in a dream, "You have accumulated many merits as a result of your sincere devotion to a true vajra-master. This is exactly what the Universal Gateway Article of the Lotus Sutra says,

> *Or, one might by an evil man be chased*
> *Down from a diamond mountain,*
> *By virtue of constant mindfulness of a Sound-*
>   *Observer*
> *He could not harm a single hair*

"Vajra Master Sheng-yen Lu is really an incarnation of Padmakumara. He came to the world with the intention of bringing happiness to humanity and releasing

117

them from their sufferings. Your escaping from harm was the result of your constantly chanting the Guru Heart Mantra. You must bow to the east to thank the Master for his compassionate help."

Lian-tsao heard his grandmother very clearly. The next morning he got up and, without any hesitation, he visualized the Master in the space to the east and started to bow twenty-one times. Then he bowed to the statue three times. Ever since he has upheld without fail the Guru Heart Mantra and the name of Amitabha.

Lian-tsao told the Master that, ever since he had enshrined the cement statue, there was peace and fewer sicknesses in the family. Although his sister was still handicapped, she started to chant the Buddha's name on her own and was happier than before. Then there was the neighbor's child who could not stop crying at night. Lian-tsao used the "rice clothes" method, in which he put some of the child's clothing on top of some rice on a tray and stuck incense in the middle. This was to absorb the fear. Miraculously, the child stopped crying at night.

In addition, due to the effectiveness of the "Cement Master," neighbors started to find out about the statue. Not only did it cure children's fears, it also cured older people's illnesses. There was an elderly woman who had been sick and bedridden for two years; her legs had become feeble. Her family used the "rice clothes" method in front of the statue. The next day, the woman could walk around.

Because there were so many people coming to pray, the statue had to be moved from the bedroom to the living room. People in the neighborhood came to make their wishes. The Cement Master started to wear more and more golden pendants around his neck as people offered the pendants to the Master when their wishes were fulfilled.

The villagers did not know what kind of deity the statue actually was. Some thought it was the Ksitigarbha Bodhisattva, some thought it was the Kitchen God, or the Taoist Master Ch'ing Shui. But Lian-tsao told them it was the Red-Crown Buddha.

Now, everyone in that village knows that there is a Red-Crown Buddha who is very efficacious and popular.

The Red-Crown Buddha is the Cement Master who is the Holy Red Crown Vajra Master, Master Sheng-yen Lu, the incarnation of Padmakumara. This legend is completely true.

The names of Lian-tsao and his village are not disclosed in this article in order to avoid too much publicity.

Amitabha!

26. The Initiation of Ghosts

Recently, we have moved our home to Redmond, Washington. The house is elegant and the atmosphere is full of joy and happiness for our family of four. Our home is decorated simply. All curtains, bed spreads and table cloths are made by my wife. Merchandise is expensive in the States; therefore, we often make things ourselves rather than purchasing them.

There is a row of trees at the back of the house. In the autumn of 1984, many leaves fell, which we soon piled up into one great heap.

I have always liked cleanliness. Whenever things become a little bit untidy, I go and tidy them up. I wipe the table if it's spotted, I pick up pieces of paper from the floor and put them into the garbage bin. My life is simple and practical. I have always done the sweeping, watering and tidying myself.

Since we moved to Redmond, Fo-ch'ing and Fo-ch'i have grown up a lot. They are very lovely and vivacious. When practice time comes, everyone meets at the True Buddha Tantric Quarter to do our cultivation. All of us, young and old, practice together. Having heard and practiced much, the children are beginning to understand the Truth of the Buddhist teachings.

In my daily practice at the new residence, I still make "offerings" to the gods and ghosts. I have also invited all the gods and ghosts from my old house to the new residence and set up a separate altar for them. Each day, at a fixed hour, I make a food offering to them. I have

120

also gone to Seattle's coast to summon the ghosts in the ocean and, as a result, many sea spirits have come to take refuge in the Holy Red Crown Vajra Master Lian-shen.

The relationship between the Master and the ghost students is harmonious. The relationship between a living person and a disembodied spirit depends on their affinity and is not affected by the fact that they are dwelling in different dimensions. If I treat the spirits well, naturally they will treat me well. This is a mutual Cause and Effect. In this respect, it is very difficult for many people to understand the true meaning. Even some Dharma teachers have mistaken the Holy Red Crown Vajra Master to be a person who keeps ghosts for personal gain, thus labeling me the "evil master," "spirit master," "demon master," and "ghost master."

Every day students from both the living world and the nether world come to take refuge. Like stars in the sky, the number of students in the disembodied realm are too numerous to count.

Autumn came. One evening I saw the fallen leaves on the ground and made a mental note to myself to clear them up early in the morning. When I got up the next morning and looked outside, I found the whole backyard was completely cleaned up! Not a single leaf remained. The great pile of leaves had been completely blown away by the wind. During the autumn, the trees shed their leaves gradually, day by day, until winter arrives. By winter, all the leaves have fallen and only naked branches remain.

But, during the whole autumn, the backyard remained clean. The leaves that fell in the daytime disappeared overnight. Sometimes, they were swept into one heap, as if someone had piled them up.

As a matter of fact, I know that every night ghosts

came. There was a ghost king who, with pale face and jutting teeth, tall and big and garbed in white, his head reaching to the heavens and his feet on earth, helped the Master to clean the front and back yards with a group of ghosts. They knew I was very busy. So, "when master is busy, students will run the errand." As a result, I did not have to take care of the yard during the entire autumn-winter period.

My neighbors on either side had to sweep up the fallen leaves on their lawns every day. They said, "The power of Master Lu has resulted in no fallen leaves at his house."

In fact, I knew there were plenty of leaves on the ground! It was just that they were cleared up by the ghost students.

There was also another incident. This was how it happened:

My wife, Fo-ch'ing, Fo-ch'i, and I were driving to downtown Seattle. While we were on Hwy 502, I suddenly smelled smoke. I was wondering what it was when, in a flash, I heard a ghost student in the sky telling me, "The stove was not turned off."

Ah! It was indeed a serious matter if the stove was not turned off. As one knows, many houses in the States are built of wood, which easily catch fire. Leaving the gas stove on the whole day could have resulted in the house being gone when we got back.

At the next exit on the highway, I turned back.

"What happened?" My wife asked.

"The stove was not turned off," I replied.

"I did actually turn it off completely," my wife said.

"You always say so; in fact you did not. What a muddle head."

My wife is famous for being muddle headed. But, I

am always very careful with everything. I always check all the lights and doors at night.

"Let's bet on this," she replied.

"All right," I said.

When we got home, the water in the kettle had completely evaporated and the bottom of the kettle had melted. Perhaps, in a while, the whole kettle might have gone. Not only that, the whole house could have been reduced to ashes. This could have been very serious! The four of us might suddenly have ended up homeless.

I told my wife it was a serious matter.

But she did not care. Wasn't everything all right? After all, with me here, she could just sit back and relax.

These ghost students have become my housekeepers. Whenever there is an emergency, they inform me. They are very accurate. They have also become my great helpers. When there are visitors to the house, they immediately know the motives of these people. They play mischief on people with bad intentions, to frighten them away so they won't return.

All these ghost students also join in our group practice sessions. Every one of them has its own Personal Deity. They can listen to the teachings while suspended in the air or while clinging to the leaves of house plants. Every one of them has also received the initiation empowerment. They help the Holy Red Crown Vajra Master in spreading the teachings.

The Holy Red Crown Vajra Master practices the Dzogchen (Complete Perfection Tantra), so everything is complete perfection. I not only save human beings, I also save all disembodied spirits. All of the ghosts recite the name of the Master and wholeheartedly chant the Guru Heart Mantra to get rid of all worries. The spiritual responses from the Padmakumara are unimaginable.

Even spirits come to take refuge in the Master to liberate themselves. The Master taught them to chant: "Om ah hum, guru bei, ah-ho-sa-sa-ma-ha, Lian-shen siddhi hum."

27. A Collection of Mystical Experiences From Students

1) Empowerment

I have received the certificate of initiation and the teaching of the **Four Preliminary Practices**. After the empowerment, I had a mystical experience. The first day at 1:00 a.m., I smelled the fragrance of sandalwood in the whole room and there were strong golden lights flashing in the air. The next day at 3:00 a.m., I smelled the fragrance and again saw the flashing of golden lights. I knew this was the empowerment of Master and was glad to receive it. Master's power is unlimited; we are so fortunate to be your students.

Lian-kung
Hong Kong

2) Job Seeking

On the same day I received Master's letter, I had an early morning dream about Master. In the dream, my family and I gathered around the Master, listening to his teachings. After that, I rushed forward with the intention of requesting guidance on job seeking. Before I opened my mouth, Master had already stretched out his right hand and gently led me by my left hand to the eleven o'clock position of a big round clock, saying that this was the place. I considered this to be the five-minutes-to-twelve o'clock position, and that it must mean that the problem of unemployment would be over very soon.

The next morning about ten o'clock, I received a letter from Ai-sheng International Brokerage Ltd., asking me to attend an interview. The following day I went to see them and was hired. Later, I found out the company's logo (as shown on the attached company letterhead) was a circle with three indentations, one of which was exactly located at the five-minutes-to-twelve o'clock position. This matched the dream completely. Master's empowerment is unimaginable!

Lian-chou
Republic of China

3) Sickness

Last month, I received Master's reply and the three charms dated November 20th. It was redirected to me upon my request by Dharma brother, Lian-ch'i from Kuala Lumpur. I am grateful for Master's compassion and for curing my second child, Mu-yao Ch'en, of his serious illness. My gratitude is inexpressible. I immediately used the charms according to your instructions. Three weeks later, my son got much better, much healthier, and manifested the effect of Master's empowerment. I am filled with admiration for the Master, and I would especially like to thank you.

Hu-ch'ing Ch'en
Malaysia

4) Initiation

Thank you, Master, for not forsaking me. Last year on August 15th, I received my certificate of initiation and became a student. This is the greatest glory of my life. Two days before I received your letter, I saw Master in a dream saying to me, "You are my student now." Indeed, two days later, I received the certificate. Master is really today's Living Buddha, answering me immediately.

I started to practice the Guru Yoga, according to your guidance. I had mystical experiences too! When reading Master's books, especially *Tantric Magic: A Collection*, the mudras on the book emitted sparkling lights. I was very surprised. Your books are really valuable and mystical. It is great fortune for people to be able to read them. Master has compassion for all beings and helps them by writing books. There is a strong feeling in me that makes me want to tell all the people in the world to read your books, to take refuge in you and practice the right Dharma, so as not to waste this lifetime.

Lian-chi
(Mei-hu Lin)
Republic of China

5) Prize Winning

I have worn the *Prize Winning Charm* written by Master and it was incredible. Within three weeks, I won the first prize of the "thousand-number ticket," winning about two thousand dollars. I was very happy because it was the first time I've won a jackpot or had that much money. Thank you, Master.

Lian-sui
(Yu-pin Wong)
Malaysia

6) Headache

As a result of Master's help, the headaches which Dharma sister, Lian-je, has had for the last thirty years or so, were cured without medication. My mother has no religious belief but, after listening to me talking about the meritorious deeds and the spiritual books of Master, she was impressed and requested to take refuge. I am writing on her behalf and hope Master will accept her.

Lian-jung
Brazil

7) Back Pain

Six years ago, I read the book, *How to Awaken One's Spirit.* I have since visited the Master at your former residence, requesting help in the healing of my chronic back pain. At that time, Master only gave me two charms, one for washing, the other for ingesting. Master also instructed me to eat boiled spinach for a week. By simply doing what was prescribed, my illness was cured.

Chi-lung Fu
Republic of China

8) Vision of Light

One night about two months ago, I did my practices according to the methods taught on pages 158, 159, and 160 of *Attaining Realization Through Sitting Meditation.* I did my practices with my palms closed, while I visualized the Master. Suddenly I saw very bright golden stars emanating from Master's forehead, radiating towards me. In my visualization, I tried to see the Dharma Body of Master, but I could only see the golden lights. After a while, I started quietly chanting the Guru Heart Mantra. I chanted it one hundred eight times. The light gradually disappeared. This was indeed a very wonderful experience. I was very delighted and would sincerely like to tell you so.

Lian-ch'i
(Tsu-lieh Ch'en)
Malaysia

9) Chanting of the Heart Mantra

Whenever I chanted: "Om ah hum, guru bei, ah-ho-sa-sa-ma-ha, Lian-shen siddhi hum," Master appeared in the space. This wonderful scene happened over and over again. Master's forehead emitted a white light onto my face, red light from his throat to mine, and blue light from his chest to mine. When the lights were on me, I had an indescribable, blissful sensation.

We live in the small town of Mindanou. Although there is a bookstore, they only sell stationery. Recently, I discovered that they have started selling Master's books. So, I bought eight of them. The first day we practiced the Guru Yoga, we had the mystical experience.

Lian-huan, Lian-yao
Malaysia

10) Healing of a Sprain

After reading the book *A Little Taste of Zen*, I am deeply respectful of the Master for suffering in the place of his students and reducing their negative karmas, as recorded in the chapter, "Seven Days of Buddha's Bleeding." I remember during the time period mentioned in the book, I was also ill. I am grateful and will never forget Master's help.

Recently, I sprained a muscle. I placed the statue of the Medicine Buddha on the altar and my condition got a little better. I also placed Master's Dharma picture on the altar and, immediately, I could move freely again. (I thought perhaps this meant I was closer to Master than to the Medicine Buddha.)

Last year, in Taipei, there was a particularly heavy rainfall. The water rose a foot high. I was, at that time, at the suburban Holy South Temple. So I prayed, and the rain stopped. I used the praying method according to your book.

The daughter of my friend's colleague was also a student of yours. When she was very sick, she continued practicing the Dharma and became well. This friend of mine used to criticize Master's writing of mystical experiences. I responded that, as Buddhists, we should offer testimony on Buddhism. He told me that, indeed, the reason for his studying Buddhism was because of reading Master's books. Recently, I ran into this friend and he, acting differently than before, praised Master as being wonderful. He even went on to say he found some other Dharma masters to be lacking in substance!

Lian-t'ung
Republic of China

11) Guru Yoga

On January 19th, I practiced the Guru Yoga. At the time of merging, my body tremored lightly and the ground shook as if there were an earthquake. When I entered into meditation, I saw my body becoming white and giving out lights, and there was the continuous sound of mantra, as if I had done it in my past life. The energy reached the top of my head as if I were receiving empowerment.

On January 20th, I practiced the Personal Deity Yoga together with the Guru Yoga. After entering into samadhi, I saw a vision in which two pillars of fire rose up next to me, or two lamps arced up like a rainbow. For the last several days, my body has felt warm, and I see light but have no visions.

I now understand that I should not be happy at the sight of lights, should not be afraid at the sight of visions, and that I must not be attached to these. These are the Master's instructions.

Lian-luo
(Hsiu-li Chang)
Republic of China

12) Lucid Dream

In a dream I saw Master coming to my new residence. I was very happy. Master's face looked just like the Dharma picture, but he was wearing casual attire. When I saw Master, I felt as if I saw my own relative and I started crying. Master said, "I'll come to see you again."

When my father bought a new house, he was short of funds. I prayed to the Padmakumara and, in the afternoon, someone came and lent money to my mother. Therefore, we had adequate funds to buy the new house. I actually saw the image of Padmakumara sitting on a lotus. His left hand was holding a lotus and he was wearing a Five Buddha Crown.

Lian-kao
(Po-wen Chang)
Republic of China

28. Cancer On The Neck

Everyone is afraid of death (except real acharyas). Sick people all desire to stay alive, as the survival instinct is one of the strongest of human instincts. It is sad when a patient with an incurable disease is informed by the doctors that there is nothing more they can do, especially when requests for continued treatment and hospitalization are turned down. Isn't this pitiful? Isn't this like a death sentence? Such was the case of a person, and the firm growth on his neck had already begun to bulge out.

After the diagnosis, the doctors told him the cancer cells had already spread to the brain. The man could no longer move his neck. In extreme agony, he thought that death was his only resort. He knew that even the preacher of his church had died of cancer. Yet God! He despised it! He wouldn't believe it!

While he was walking down the street, he happened to come across a Chinese bookstore. He walked inside and looked around. Strangely, one of the books seemed to have light coming out of it. He reached for this book and started reading it. It looked like a book about Tantra as well as philosophy. The book was *A Little Taste of Zen.*

He would not believe in these things at all! What was this "Seven Days of Buddha's Bleeding," attaining happiness and release from suffering? It said if the practitioner had confidence it would eliminate bad karmas and sickness? And what was this "internal fire" practiced by Dr. Chieh Wen? It said that hepatitis, the hardening of the liver, could be cured and that one could become a completely new person. The vajra master in Seattle ... what was a vajra master? He did not understand at all.

Why did Ph.D.'s and physicians take refuge in this vajra master? When the man saw the address in the book, he copied it down. Curious, he wrote a letter with only a few sentences: "When I saw your book, I felt good. A person who suffers from cancer, knowing that he is not far from death, hopes for protection or release from sufferings. I would also request an initiation empowerment from the vajra master."

Soon after the letter was sent, the man dreamed he was walking into a big house where many people were listening to a preacher. That preacher had a golden body and was wearing a Five Buddha Crown. He looked magnificent. He was also the vajra master pictured in the book. That vajra master waved to him and said, "Lian-fan, your illness is the result of your previous life karmas! You must recite the Guru Heart Mantra. The Master will cure your illness." "Lian-fan" walked up in front of the master, who then smeared his neck with pure, clean water. Strangely, he felt cool and comfortable. The neck didn't feel as stiff and hard anymore. He was very grateful and knelt down immediately, bowing to the vajra master. At this point "Lian-fan" woke up. But, he still felt the pain on his neck and he had not been cured. He thought the dream was probably a reflection of his hopes.

But, a strange thing happened again. He received his Certificate of Initiation and his refuge-name *was* exactly Lian-fan! On that same night, he had another strange dream. He again walked into the same big house where many people were listening to the vajra master delivering a discourse. The vajra master transformed until he was immensely tall and emitting golden rays of light. Lian-fan was kneeling down on the floor and sincerely bowing

133

to the Master.

He said to the Master, "The neck hasn't healed."

The Master said, "You must chant the Guru Heart Mantra confidently."

Again the master smeared his neck with pure, cool water. Once again, he felt very soothed and he woke up after that.

Lian-fan thought, since he had already had the same dream twice, why not try to chant the mantra wholeheartedly? No matter what, it was better than waiting to die. So he determined to put everything else aside and, whenever he was free, he would chant the Guru Heart Mantra. He did it even when he was walking or riding in a car, both in the morning and at night.

Strangely enough, after he started chanting, he was able to turn his neck. The bulge on his neck began to subside day by day. Finally one day, when he looked in the mirror, everything was back to normal. The date the doctors had surmised to be Lian-fan's last, passed and Lian-fan seemed to be recovering. His complexion changed from yellow and white to a lustrous pink. This was just like a fairy tale come true.

He went back to the doctors for a checkup. The doctors repeatedly exclaimed that this was strange, the cancer cells were gone completely! The doctors just could not believe the mantra would cure the sickness.

But Lian-fan was definitely cured.

Lian-fan swore to himself that as long as he lived, he would be willing to contribute his strength to spread the Tantric teachings of the True Buddha School, telling people the good news of how he was cured and hoping other people would take refuge in the Holy Red Crown Vajra Master.

The Guru Heart Mantra is able to supercede negative

karma. This was another great miracle. Only a real vajra master has the ability to accomplish such miracles.

Lian-fan is the "Lian-fan" who resides in Belgium.

29. Messages From Chicago

Venerable Master Lu:

The last time I left Chicago, it was stormy and snowing. Chicago is the well-known "Wind City" of the United States. The plane was unable to take off, even after two attempts. Many people were frightened but I was calm as usual because it was the first time that I was going to meet the Holy Red Crown Vajra Master Lian-shen, the Illustrious Acharya. If something wrong was going to happen, Bodhisattva Lian-shen would have prevented me from going in the first place. Finally, at the third attempt, the plane took off and soared into the clouds. Everyone applauded and cheered. I was grateful for the care of Bodhisattva Lian-shen.

Looking out of the plane from the skies above Chicago, it was flat for hundreds of miles in all directions. There wasn't a mountain or even a hill that I could see. However, when we were above Salt Lake City, I was transfixed to see the continuous mountain ranges. It was January the 5th when I landed in Seattle, where there were unbroken mountain ranges edged by the ocean, coupled with thin fogs that gently encircled the slopes. Streaks of white snow lay everywhere. The blue of the sea joined the azure sky canopy. It was difficult for people to know whether they were in the sky or on the land. No wonder master praised: "The geographical spiritual energy of Seattle is the most exuberant in the U.S.."

With the instructions given by Mrs. Lu over the phone, I rented a car at the airport, headed for Highway

405, and drove for about one hour, enjoying the scenery on the way. Entering the city of Redmond, I stopped by a flower shop on top of a hill, where many people were enjoying the flowers. A girl was busily walking in and out of the shop; I asked her where Master Lu lived. Everyone started to point to the west where there were a few houses. Just looking at the houses, and without anybody telling me, I knew the one with a red roof and white walls was the residence of Master. I felt there was spiritual energy spreading out in all directions. This was:

Red rays beaming up, reaching the heavens,
White walls shining to all directions;
Spiritual energy soaring millions of yards,
Enveloping the realm of the human world.
Where is the divine place of the great immortal?
Simply look towards Seattle; the number one divine
place is there.

Once I entered the house, I felt an atmosphere of warmth and friendliness. Fo-ch'ing and Fo-ch'i came up and said, "Master is upstairs." I knew Master could be in meditation and I did not dare disturb him. So, I went first to the altar and bowed to all Buddhas and Bodhisattvas. Dharma brother Hung and his family from Vancouver, Canada were also there. Together in the sitting-room, we viewed the pictures of Buddhas and Bodhisattvas on the wall. Suddenly, I felt rays of energy approaching. I looked up — it was Master coming down the stairs. Suddenly I was at a loss what to do. I hurriedly joined my palms and bowed to Master and said, "I am Yang Chen-chia from Chicago. I've come to pay homage to the Master." Master replied, saying, "I know you."

After seeing Master, I realized that the spiritual energy radiating light from Master's face was so strong that it shone like a big star at night. Green, white, gold, and yellow lights converged into a bright and radiating light. Especially in group sessions, Master was like the sun and the rest of us became little fireflies and stars.

I am grateful for the Master's loving care in personally empowering me. I felt a current of energy entering me and cleansing my negative karmas. My body felt light and floating, and I had a flying sensation. In my meditation, I reached the samadhi stage, which made me understand the greatness of the Master.

Master has already attained "the key to secrets " and "vajra samadhi" and, therefore, has the compassionate heart of a Bodhisattva as well as the diamond quality that can get rid of millions of problems. His power of mental concentration is unparalleled, because he did not have to wait for me to ask questions to answer them for me. I felt he was extremely effective.

That evening in the regular group practice, I met many young Americans who bowed to the Master with reverence. To my understanding, they have extremely deep knowledge of Buddhist teachings. Perhaps in the future, they will be the Dharma teachers who will propagate Buddhist teachings throughout America.

I saw Master's spiritual light moving around, and was stunned and speechless to watch the hundreds and thousands of different mudras he displayed. How many years would it take for ordinary people like us to learn these several thousand kinds of mudras? The hand manipulations were absolutely wonderful, and their purpose was beyond the comprehension of laymen.

After I returned to Chicago, I found it was still covered in snow. The wind was chilly, but my heart was a ball of fire. As a matter of fact, the thing that made me happiest and most excited was Master's empowerment and his patience in teachings. That night, after a few minutes of meditation, I had a mystical experience. I felt my crown chakra open up and saw a ray of white and red light passing in front of me. From the top of my crown, Master descended, entered my body, and sat on a lotus in my heart. My inner spirit started to become activated. I felt a happiness that was hard to express. Here is a verse:

The gate to Heaven has been unlocked,
Good deeds and cultivation are the True Ways;
Master is indeed unparalleled in the past and present,
One howl breaks up the illusion of thousands of life-
times.

Last night and the night before, I did my usual meditation and recited the name of the Holy Red Crown Vajra Master Sheng-yen Lu. After about fifteen minutes, I saw a ray of white light coming down from the sky, inducing my true spirit to move. In each practice, I felt the presence of the master. I shall be grateful and delighted, forever and ever.

I would like to offer another verse to pay homage to the Master:

Receiving empowerment from the Red Crown Vajra
Master,
I vow to follow the master to the nether world;
Never receding with the vows of Bodhisattva Ksiti-
garbha,
Until all beings attain Buddhahood.

Yang Chen-chia
Student

"Messages from Chicago" was written by a student who came for the first time to my house requesting initiation and empowerment. Yang Chen-chia came to the United States many years ago as a foreign student and had obtained a doctorate degree. After wandering extensively in the world, he finally decided to take refuge in me. Buddhas and Bodhisattvas have compassion for him and have reached out their hands to him.

During the last half year, the number of visitors from all over has increased, and many of them have doctorate degrees. They've all received empowerments from the Holy Red Crown Vajra Master and learned the vast and profound Dharma of the Heart. Every letter they have written contain remarks of respect and great praise. Everyone has had a mystical experience. Therefore, the mystical experience of Buddha Dharma is really authentic.

Due to the volume of letters, I chose one, Yang Chen-chia's letter, to offer as evidence of mystical experience.

"Messages from Chicago" was the personal experience of Yang Chen-chia. It was written with real feeling. All phenomena are the results of the mind. Everyone should understand this and pursue the Buddhist teachings.

30. The Proper Name of the True Buddha Home Temple

In regard to the True Buddha School's Home Temple, I must make the following clear to all students:

The address of the Home Temple is:

17102 N.E. 40 Ct,

Redmond, Washington 98052

U.S.A.

The location of the Home Temple was selected by me some years ago, after trekking the whole of the United States. The chosen geography had "dragon energies" at the back, mountains in front, and a lake before the mountains. The landscape is protected by the geographical features surrounding it. Looking in the distance from the Home Temple one can see the mountains and waters unfolding in all their majesty, as well as the abundant white clouds, all resembling the scene of heaven.

The Home Temple was originally a grass hill. The dragon vein [Feng-shui terminology] had formed into dragon dens here, which were marked by three old, huge pine trees. After the place had been chosen, it was immediately purchased by a group of eight students. The main shrine for the Home Temple was to be built over the main dragon den.

There were various difficulties in getting building permits from the state government and the City of Redmond. The neighboring residents opposed it. Ministers and lawyers together opposed it. During the course of three years and twelve hearings, the problems were settled one by one. The court recognized that what we were going to do was legal, despite oppositions from neighbors, ministers and lawyers. Finally, we won the battle.

Our final success was due to help from American friends and lawyers, arrangements for community friendship meetings to resolve differences, and having influential people to speak for us. It was also due to our hard struggle and firm stand.

Building a temple in Redmond, Washington, U.S.A. was not an easy task for the True Buddha disciples who had came from Taiwan, especially when we were surrounded by "territories" of Catholics, Protestants and Mormons. However, we finally made it, paying with our blood and tears. Imagine, twelve court hearings! How many people could go through this?

On March 28th, 1985, the crane came to install the sign of the Home Temple. It was drizzling as the final construction was underway. Watching the finished walls, we were so moved and overjoyed that we were unable to distinguish between rain and tears.

The construction of the Home Temple was originally supposed to go through bids, which were generally very expensive. The total construction cost was half a million U.S. dollars. Where was the money going to come from? We couldn't imagine where the money would come from. Our funds came from three sources: generous donations from the wealthy, smaller donations from all the students, and the funds acquired from the previous five ceremonies performed by the Master. That totaled about one hundred thousand U.S. dollars.

So, we adopted special solutions. We had Master Chen Sen-he to take charge of the construction. He had extensive experience in construction work and was skillful in electrical wiring and plumbing. He was also familiar with all materials and knew all the construction workers. We acted as our own contractor, purchased the materials, hired people, subcontracted to others, and tried to save where we could. On plumbing and electrical wiring, we tried to do the job ourselves wherever possible. We even did the excavation and sewer system, and erected the wall framework. The funds were still insufficient, but we believed as long as we had the materials, we would complete the building no matter what. The deficit funds would be acquired later by some other means.

Now, the Home Temple is already half finished. Our plan is to complete it in 1985. Even if there is not enough money, we will still apply our manpower to accomplish it.

In the future, the proper names would be as follows:

1) "Rey Tseng Temple": This refers to the main temple that is being built. The temple is the biggest of our buildings. In the main hall of the temple, there will be the shrine of Kuan-yin Bodhisattva in the middle, the Taoist Golden Mother of the Primordial Pond on the right, and the Ksitigarbha Bodhisattva on the left. On the left and right of the main hall are two side halls which can be used for any other functions. If there is a ceremony, temporary lodging could be set up there. They are fully equipped with kitchen, washroom, bathroom, and utilities. In the future, ceremonies and group practice will be held at the Rey Tseng Temple. Modeled after the classical Chinese temples, the finished temple will have an authentic quaint look with golden roof tiles and red pillars.

2) "Ling Shen Ching Tze": In front of the Rey Tseng Temple, there are four houses on each side and a main, private road in between. There is a cement wall, the only one in the City of Redmond, surrounding the whole area. These eight houses, as well as many other houses nearby, are all occupied by True Buddha School disciples. The area that includes the eight houses (in two rows), the

143

main private road between them, and the temple is called "Ling Shen Ching Tze." In the future, the symbol for Ling Shen Ching Tze will be placed in front of the main entrance. The Ling Shen Ching Tze, being a community of the Home Temple, will provide the foundation for the future True Buddha College.

3) The formal title of the Home Temple is *True Buddha School Ling Shen Ching Tze Rey Tseng Temple*. True Buddha disciples may address the Home Temple by its title or they can simply use Home Temple of the True Buddha School. Rey Tseng Temple is the main temple at Ling Shen Ching Tze.

4) "True Buddha Tantric Quarter": This is the Tantric altar of Holy Red Crown Vajra Master, where he usually practices. All rituals and group practices are carried out at the Rey Tseng Temple and private practices are at the True Buddha Tantric Quarter. The group empowerments for students will be held at the temple, while secret empowerments will be at the True Buddha Tantric Quarter.

— Founder of the True Buddha School — The Holy Red Crown Vajra Master Sheng-yen Lu, the Tantrika.

— Abbot of the Rey Tseng Temple — Master Lianhuo.

— Assistant Abbot of the Rey Tseng Temple — Master Lian-shih.

This True Buddha School will, in the future, propagate Buddhist teachings in the world. The number of masters (teachers) will reach over two hundred. All teachers must come here personally to receive the teachings and the acharya empowerment from the Holy Red Crown Vajra Master. Acharya certificates will be issued to them. It is hoped that all students will generate the Bodhicitta and be able to achieve self-realization, and, together, spread the Tantric teachings.

Right now, there are 70,000 students[1] all over the world. In the future, more teachers will appear, and the Buddha Dharma will spread throughout the world.

In principle, those who practice the Tantra of this School and who want results, must abide and respect what is written on the initiation certificate; that is, they must have strong confidence in the founder of the School and his teachings, and they must practice persistently. This is what Padmasambhava emphasized: "Honor the guru, treasure the Dharma, and practice diligently."

The True Buddha School does not discriminate against other sects or religions. All religious teachings have their own merits. All sects have their own uniqueness. True Buddha School's teachings consist of Taoism, Sutrayana, and Tantra, and range from the basic to the highest levels, depending on the karmic causes of the students. There is also the supreme Highest Yoga to be taught by the truly enlightened Master, enabling one to achieve Buddhahood within one's lifetime. All of these are genuine and can be proved. Also, the lineage is genuine. People who want to learn the Vajrayana should take refuge in the truly Great Enlightened Vajra Master.

---

[1] As of 1993, the number of True Buddha disciples exceeds 1,000,000.

31. The Worldly Dharma and the Transcendental Dharma

On Monday, March 25th, 1985, at seven o'clock in the evening, there was a private party at Mr. Chieh-jen Wang's house. The guest of honor was Commissioner Yü-chü Ch'en of the Seattle branch of the Public Affairs Division of Taiwan, Coordination Council for North American Affairs. The Chen brothers and I were also invited.

It came to my knowledge that, when the commissioner and his wife were married in Hopeh Province, Mr. Wang's mother-in-law (Mrs. K'ang) had presided over the wedding ceremony. At that time, there was a custom to do the "Bedspread" formality. It was conducted by Mrs. K'ang during which she had to speak phrases associated with auspiciousness, such as "early arrival of children" and the like. Mrs. K'ang and Commissioner Ch'en came from the same village in Hopeh. Since Mrs. K'ang was visiting the United States, she had invited the commissioner over to chat about the old days.

Since I have been here in the States for three years, all the people in the Coordination Council know me. The head consul and the other consuls have become very good friends of mine. After the conversation started, everybody was relaxed and at ease. Around the table there were only the two Chen brothers, Commissioner and Mrs. Ch'en, Mr. Wang Chieh-jen, Mrs. K'ang, and myself, seven in all. Mrs. Wang Chieh-jen cooked the dinner.

During dinner, Mr. and Mrs. Ch'en asked many questions, especially Mrs. Ch'en, who believed very much in karma and reincarnation. She had a great affinity with Buddhas and a great root of wisdom.

"Where will Master be teaching?" Commissioner Ch'en asked.

"This April 4th, I will be going to Hong Kong, Brunei, and Malaysia. My plan is to visit three countries every year, to teach and to see for myself those students in each country."

"What are the Worldly Dharma and Transcendental Dharma in Buddhism?" asked the Commissioner.

"The Worldly Dharma of Buddhism deals with the worldly affairs of living beings. It is the Dharma that enters into the life of worldly beings to release their sufferings. For example, methods for curing sickness, for long life, for children, wealth and happiness in the family, are all Worldly Dharma. However, though the Buddhist Worldly Dharma is a Dharma for worldly affairs, it is also concerned with getting rid of the three poisons (greed, anger, and ignorance), practicing the **Five Precepts**, carrying out the **Ten Wholesome Actions**, and performing the Six Perfections (paramitas). The Worldly Dharma is the foundation of the Transcendental Dharma. The Transcendental Dharma is the method of evolving beyond the world, that is, to break up the illusion and to seek realization. The Transcendental Dharma is the true practice that leads one to attain Buddhahood, to leave the world and reach the realm of No Birth and No Extinction. The Transcendental Dharma does not seek reputation, benefit, children, or long life. There is only one goal, to transcend Life and Death and become a Buddha. This is the Transcendental Dharma."

"Is your teaching Worldly or Transcendental Dharma?"

"Both."

"Do Buddhist teachings encompass Cause and Effect, karma and transmigration?"

"Yes, *cause* is a seed which is planted, *effect* is the fruit from the seed. Thus, you reap what you sow. When we plant wheat, it's impossible to get rice. This is the meaning of Cause and Effect. Buddhism talks about Cause and Effect. We always say cause is the doer, effect is the recipient. Planting a good cause will result in a good effect; planting a bad cause will result in a bad effect. In fact, the theory about Cause and Effect is a kind of logic which is very scientific. The **Twelve Links of Cause and Effect** is a method to realize the truth of the cycles, of birth and death within the Six Realms of existence, that sentient beings have been undergoing from time immemorial. Transmigration is like a wheel, revolving endlessly. To give an example, there is not much equality at birth: some children are born in poor and undeveloped countries, some in rich and powerful countries; some are born as princes, some as beggars. Actually, these have to do with karma and transmigration and only karma and transmigration can account for the inequality."

I continued, "Some religions assert that there is no karma and transmigration. Who, then, can judge men and arbitrarily assign them to be born? In respect to transmigration, many people understand the causes in previous lives and the effects in this life. Those who have attained a higher level of practice are able to tell, upon meeting someone, in which particular realm he comes from. They can also understand this present life as well as future lives. The ability to understand Cause and Effect in the past, present, and future is the Divine Faculty of Fate."

"Can Master talk about the main idea of the Buddhist teachings?" Mrs. Ch'en asked.

"The gist of Buddhist teachings is to cultivate to become Buddhas. All human activities in the world have to do with food, clothing, housing, transportation, education, and entertainment, all of which are exterior. The so-called mortals are those who exert themselves to pursue exterior success, and this is what the Worldly Dharma deals with. But for the sages, not only do they possess the Worldly Dharma, they also pursue the inner-realization within themselves. When inner-realization is achieved, one will understand the wonderful Dharma taught by the Buddha on the karma law of the **Five Vehicles**. Buddhist teachings assert that all things are mind. The mind is within oneself and, therefore, it is called inner-realization. Understanding the Absolute Reality of one's own mind and obtaining the Truth of an inner-realization are the important goals of Buddhist teachings."

Mrs. K'ang said, "What Master just said really makes sense. How enlightening!"

I said, "Not at all."

"Whenever we have foreign visitors, they all mention you. Everyone knows about you and your divination ability," said Commissioner Ch'en.

"That's right!" Agreed Mrs. Ch'en. "Are you of the Kagyu lineage?"

"Yes! I have studied the teachings of the Schools of Nyingma, Kagyu, Geluk, and Sakya. My lineage is an aggregation of many schools; however, I am not of the Black sect." I said, smiling.

"Yes? What's the Black sect?"

"The Black sect, or Bon, was originally a native religion from Tibet, before Tantra was introduced into Tibet. Therefore, Bon religion is not Tantra; all Tantric practitioners know that." I replied.

I told Commissioner and Mrs. Ch'en that Ling Shen

149

Ching Tze Rey Tseng Temple was going to open in 1985. At that time, I would invite all the officers from the Co-ordination Council to tour the place. This would be an unprecedented event in the State of Washington because the temple of the True Buddha School was built by private effort without any institutional funding.

At the same time, I would invite the Mayor of the City of Redmond and other administrators to the inauguration of the temple. All residents of the city would also be invited. At the inauguration, there would be Dharma Ceremony and parties. Students living in Ling Shen Ching Tze would welcome the guests.

"Oh! That's very good," said Commissioner and Mrs. Ch'en.

"Listening to Master Lu today, is better than reading ten years of books!"

"Not at all!" I replied.

I know Mrs. Ch'en has a great affinity for Buddhism. She understands a great deal. I believe her opportunity to learn the teachings will occur soon.

It was a very meaningful dinner party.

32. Golden Light From Ten Thousand Lotuses

This is an account of the fifth Dharma Ceremony in Tukwila, Washington, U.S.A.: —

On March 2nd, 1985, which was the 11th day of the first lunar month, the True Buddha School held a global Blessing Ceremony in Tukwila, Washington, U.S.A..

Close to a thousand students came from all over the world. Everyone wore yellow Dharma robes. In this ceremony alone, participating Dharma acharyas included Master Lian-shen, Master Lian-huo, Master Lian-shih, Master Lian-chi, Master Lian-yi, Master Lian-yüan, Master Lian-ke, Master Lian-t'ing, and Master Lian-chih — nine altogether. It could be seen that this was a magnificent and grand ceremony.

Holy Red Crown Vajra Master Lian-shen wore a Five Buddha Crown on his head, a yellow Dharma robe, a red cassock, a white jade mala on the chest, and a pair of straw sandals. Master Lian-huo and Master Lian-shih also wore Five Buddha Crowns, yellow Dharma robes, brown cassocks, and straw sandals. The Blessing Ceremony was conducted by these three Masters.

At the beginning of the ceremony, Venerable Master Lian-shen, sitting upright on the treasure throne, held a plate full of rice representing all sentient beings in the universe. With the rice under the divine light of all Buddhas and Bodhisattvas, he sincerely read the repentance prayer and called upon the Buddhas and Bodhisattvas to turn the great Dharma Wheels, so as to empower all beings with Light and to endow them with prosperity and auspiciousness.

At this moment, the power of compassion of the Buddhas and Bodhisattvas radiated to the Ten Directions. The Holy Red Crown Vajra Master Lian-shen, with many masters and even many students, saw purple lights appearing in the sky. These lights transformed into blossom after blossom of purple-golden lotuses that twirled and multiplied into thousands and tens of thousands of lotuses filling up the whole space. Like Buddhas and Bodhisattvas, these thousands and tens of thousands of lotuses endowed all beings with magnificent luminosity.

When Lian-shen the Venerable transformed, in a flash, into the State of Purity, his wonderful wisdom became united with the mind of the students. The Padmakumara was emitting Light, and there was an interflow of consciousness with the True Buddha students. This was a most magnificent moment. Many students' eyes were full of tears. John Chen cried, Hsiao-he Wang cried, Ch'ien-yi Ch'en cried, Hsin-chu Li cried, Chen-fang Luo cried, Chi-lu Chiang cried.......many, many acharyas and students cried uncontrollably.

We recited the Universal Gateway Article of the Lotus Sutra, the High King Avalokitesvara Sutra, and the mantra "Om Mani Padme Hum." Master Lian-shen displayed hundreds and thousands of mudras. Master, Buddhas, Bodhisattvas and everyone, united into one. We also respectfully recited for empowerment the divine title of Kuan-yin Bodhisattva and the heart mantras of seven other principal deities.

This kind of crying was not of sadness but, rather, of joy when the spiritual lights of the Buddhas, Bodhisattvas and the Padmakumara poured into the hearts of the believers, opening their hearts.

Lian-shen the Venerable, seated high upon the Dharma throne, empowered the True Buddha students one by one with divine water, and endowed them with peace mantras. Many students also brought Buddha statues, pictures and pendants to be empowered by the Master. The Venerable Master again recited the Great Compassion Dharani to make for every one the Great Compassion Dharani Holy Water. The water was quickly bottled and taken home by the students.

One of the outstanding features of the ceremony was that, from Ching Chü Tang [Pure Abode Chapter] and Ching Yin Tang [Pure Sound Chapter] (the Edmonton chapters in Canada), more than thirty of the students had chartered an airplane to fly to the United States to attend this ceremony. In the ceremony, they dressed uniformly in Dharma robes. Indeed, these two chapters are among the most co-operative chapters in the True Buddha School worldwide.

Another outstanding feature was that this ceremony had a great number of Westerners attending, including Lawyer Henry, an immigration officer, a professor and, a travel agent, etc., many of whom also donated funds for the building of the temple. They also received initiations and empowerments from the Master. The number of Western students has reached several thousand. Many Western scholars praised the Master highly and bowed to him. One scholar of Indian Studies said Lian-shen, the Venerable, must have seen the deva Shiva and was fit to accept the glory of the "Nine Umbrellas," which is the highest honor for a practitioner in his life.

Ten thousands lotuses emitted golden lights. Everyone was full of tears and everyone received the blessing empowerments. This was an unparalleled Blessing Ceremony. I would like to offer a verse:

Ten thousand assembled as if in a Heavenly Palace,
The manifestation of Bodhisattvas and Master was
magnificent,
Whose lotus emitted purple light and faint, scented
fog,
Endowing Brightness with extraordinary wonder.

Such a great ceremony! How unusually wonderful to have such an extraordinary mystical experience!

33. Invitation To A Speech

The following invitation letter was sent to me:

CAST — Chinese-American Association
for Science and Technology
21414-68th Ave S., Kent, WA 98032
Tel: (206)-872-8500

February 19, 1985
Mr. Sheng-yen Lu
17102 N.E. 40 St.
Redmond, WA 98052

Dear Mr. Lu:

CAST members and other local engineers and professionals hold a bimonthly informal dinner gathering. During these gatherings, interesting topics ranging from fishing to personal finance are discussed. We will feel honored if you will accept our invitation to give a talk on Thursday, March 7, 1985 at 6:00 p.m.. The place will be the China Gate Restaurant. Your dinner and transportation will be provided. Please give Dr. Koh a call at 523-9919 if you will be able to attend the gathering.

Looking forward to meeting you.

Sincerely,
Wen-Hui Jou
Secretary
WHJ:wm

The invitation from the Chinese-American Association for Science and Technology was handed to me by assistant officer in-charge, Mr. Cheng, of the Taiwan Coordination Council. At that time, I was busy with my blessing ceremony scheduled for March 2nd. But, I accepted to take part in their bi-monthly gathering and give a talk.

Of course, the members of the Science and Technology Association are all qualified scientists and technologists. Most members are intellectuals, with Ph.D. degrees. Their invitation indicated that scientists are attaching importance to the study of psychics. It also indicated that scientists also have great respect for religions.

The name Holy Red Crown Vajra Master has spread from the States to all over the world. Recently, there have been many invitations to give seminars. But, due to my "practices" and "writings," which occupy most of my time, many of the invitations could not be accepted. In this regard, I'd like to apologize for all the requests I had to refuse.

Regarding "religious power" and "spiritual energy," these have aroused the attention of many countries in the world. Currently, among the peoples that study psychic energy, the Russians are the most enthusiastic, followed by the English and the Americans. Scientists in these countries, using objective studies and analysis, have found that a mysterious force does exist. Such belief is not groundless.

Using scientific means to analyze the "mystery force" involves very strict experiments. Many authentic scientific experiments are recorded on film. For example, a physicist at Stanford University believes very much in the existence of "mind power." Another physicist of another American college also acknowledges the reality of psychic power. An English university professor, after having conducted scientific experiments for many years, came to the conclusion that some kind of a force unmistakably exists.

Are "religious power," "mind power," and "spiritual energy" in conflict with science? They are not. I know with certainty that the "exterior world" is under the manipulation of the "inner world." The exterior world is of material nature and the inner world is of spiritual nature. The material and the spiritual are Cause and Effect, relating to one another like both sides of a piece of paper that cannot be separated.

We know that *physical energy* is a kind of external phenomenon and *mental energy* is an invisible phenomenon. For example, brain waves, thoughts, etc. are invisible energies. If we human beings are able to concentrate and direct our brain waves into physical matters, altering the latter, this is the *inner world* manipulating the *outer world.*

Based on religious practice, Holy Red Crown Vajra Master, the Tantric Practitioner, during Zen meditation, uses visualization, mudra and mantra to activate man's primordial potential energy. This activation enables such energy to unite with cosmic energy, producing the great cosmic energy in man.

Religious practice is not *superstition*, rather, it is a scientific practice of *inner illumination.* The practice of Zen meditation is, indeed, a great science among the sciences.

In the world of science today, many people do not understand these principles. They only believe what they see, thinking that anything "invisible" is not science. In fact, many kinds of "energy" are invisible, such as electricity, magnetism, radiation, etc..

The Tantric practices of Master Lian-shen have proved the existence of "religious power," "mental power," and "spiritual energy." They have also turned many scientists from non-believers into believers. The invitation of the Science and Technology Association is a good indication. We have already joined the exterior in science with the interior of spirituality. This is extraordinary and inconceivable!

Glossary

Glossary

Amitabha

The Buddha of "Limitless Light." This is one of the most important and popular Buddhas of the Mahayana, the subject of the Amitabha Sutra, who presides over the Western Paradise [Sukhavati] described in the Sukhavativyuha Sutra. He is the focus of all Pure Land school devotions.

Avalokitesvara (Also Avalokita, in Chinese "Guan Yin," or "Kuan Yin.")

One of the most important Bodhisattvas of the Mahayana. The literal meaning of Avalokitesvara is "He Who Hears the Sounds [Outcries] of the World." He embodies one of the two fundamental aspects of Buddhahood: compassion, in virtue of which he is often given the epithet "Great Compassion." The other fundamental aspect of Buddhahood is wisdom, which is embodied by the Bodhisattva Manjusri. Avalokitesvara is also one of the two helpers of Amitabha Buddha in the Western Paradise (the other is Mahasthamaprapta).

Bodhisattva

In general, this term applies to anyone who has taken the vow to relinquish his or her personal enlightenment in order to work for the benefit of all sentient beings. More specifically, it designates a special class of beings who have not only taken that vow but who also have attained a significant level of realization.

Bon

Pre-Buddhist religion of Tibet.

Buddha

"Awakened One." 1) One who has purified all obscurations and perfected all good qualities. 2) Shakyamuni Buddha. 3) Celestial Awakened Ones, such as Amitabha. 4) The primordially pure nature of one's own mind.

Buddha Dharma — see Dharma

Chakra

Term for the subtle energy centers in the human energy body. The seven principal chakras are (1) Muladhara (Bottom) chakra — located at the lowest part of the central energy channel, between the root of the genitals and the anus. (2) Svadhishthana (Genital) chakra — located in the central energy channel at the root of the genitals. (3) Manipura (Navel) chakra — located within the central energy channel in the region of the navel. (4) Anahata (Heart) chakra — located in the heart region within the central energy channel. (5) Vishuddha (Throat) chakra — located at the lower end of the throat. (6) Ajna (Brow Point) chakra — located in the space between the eyebrows. (7) Sahasrara (Crown) chakra — located at top of the crown of the head.

Charm

"Fu-lu." Chinese magical talismans used by many schools of religious Taoism. Fu-lu are strips of paper inscribed with symbols that resemble Chinese writing. They protect the wearer against illness and ward off demons.

Deva

A long-lived celestial being or god.

Dharma

"That which is firmly established." The doctrine and path taught by the Buddha. Truth.

Dharma Body — see Three Bodies.

Divine Hearing — see Six Transcendental Powers.

Feng Shui

"Wind and water." The study of the spiritual energy of a geographical area; geomancy.

Five Precepts

Refrain from killing; refrain from taking intoxicants; refrain from committing adultery; refrain from engaging in double talk or gossip; refrain from stealing.

Five Vehicles

Method for entering the realms of humans, heavens, Sravaka, Pratyeka-Buddhas and Bodhisattvas.

Four Preliminary Practices

The practices of Great Homage, Mandala Offerings, Fourfold Refuge, and Vajrasattva.

Karma

1) "Causality." The Law of the Universe; as one sows, so shall one reap, independent of personal belief systems or expectations. The basis of all Buddhist teaching, it is infallible but operates on many levels at once. 2) "Action." Acts of one's body, speech, mind and/or the phenomenal world which, being one in nature, are completely interdependent.

Karmic — Adjective of karma.

Maha

Great, huge.

Mahamudra

One of the highest teachings of the Vajrayana which, in Tibet, is transmitted especially in the Kagyupa school.

Mala

A string of beads that is used to count repetitions in the recitation of mantras, and the name of Buddha. The number of beads in a Buddhist mala is 108.

Mantra

A power-laden syllable or series of syllables that manifests certain cosmic forces and aspects of the Buddhas. Sometimes also the name of a Buddha.

Mara

"Destroyer." Any foe or obstacle to inner purification and maturation. Shakyamuni Buddha graphically described an onslaught of "Lord Mara's armies" as being seductive, confusing, and terrifying. However, by remaining in samadhi (deep meditation), he completely penetrated all separateness and awakened to primordial awareness. In Buddhist medicine, any mental poison, physical sickness, or psychic attack is a "mara."

Mudra

Hand gesture that accompanies the performance of liturgies and the recitation of mantras.

Naga

The "dragon." A water deity who lives in the sea.

Padmakumara

"Lotus child." The Bodhisattva(s) who resides in the Maha Twin Lotus Ponds in the Western Paradise.

Paramitas

"Means to reach the other shore." The transcendental. The paramitas, generally translated as "the perfections," are the virtues perfected by a Bodhisattva in the course of his development. There are six of these, see Six Perfections.

Sadhana

Manual of practice of deity yoga.

Samadhi

Meditative concentration/stabilization.

Six Perfections

(1) Generosity, giving; (2) discipline; (3) patience; (4) energy or exertion; (5) meditation; (6) wisdom.

Six Realms [Six Paths]

Six aspects of samsara, whether experienced subjectively or objectively. These are Hell Being (torture), Hungry Ghost (craving), Animal (stupidity), Human (insecurity), Fighting Demigod (jealousy), and Samsaric God (pride). The latter two are advantageous, but limited. Only in the human realm can one effectively cultivate to Buddhahood.

Six Transcendental Powers

The six supernatural powers mentioned in Buddhism are: (1) divine vision (instantaneous view of anything, anywhere, in the form-realm); (2) divine hearing (perception of human and divine voices); (3) perception of the thoughts of other beings; (4) recollection of previous existences; (5) divine speed (power to be anywhere at will); (6) knowledge concerning the extinction of one's own impurities and passions, which signifies with certainty of having attained liberation.

Tantra

"Weaving." Refers to esoteric spiritual teaching, specifically Buddhist Yoga, in the form of 1) ritual initiation text, 2) meditation discipline, or 3) class of teachings on transforming awareness. By connotation, the term refers to the inseparability of Buddha nature, Buddhist yoga, and Realization.

Tantrika

"Practitioner of Tantra." Someone who has formally received Buddhist Refuge and full initiation into a Tantra by an authorized guru. A Tantrika is principally concerned with enacting enlightened awareness by identifying himself or herself with an enlightened being, as opposed to studying the causes of enlightenment as given in the sutras.

Tathagata

"Thus Gone One." Synonym for Buddha. Tathagatagarbha refers to the primordially pure Buddha nature which can neither be created anew nor ever destroyed. However, this nature can remain obscured indefinitely if not purified and developed.

Ten Wholesome Actions

The ability to give up forever killing, stealing, sexual misconduct, lying, slandering, harsh language, frivolous speech, lust, hate and wrong views.

Three Bodies [Trikaya]

Refers to the three bodies possessed by a Buddha, according to the Mahayana view. The basis of this teaching is the conviction that a Buddha is one with the absolute, and he manifests in the relative world in order to work for the welfare of all beings. The three bodies are: 1. Dharmakaya (Dharma Body, body of the great order); the true nature of the Buddha, which is identical with transcendental reality, the essence of the universe. 2. Sambhogakaya (Bliss Body, body of delight); the manifestation in dreams, visions, and divine realms. 3. Nirmanakaya (Transformation Body); the earthly body in which Buddhas appear to men, in order to fulfill the Buddhas' resolve to guide all beings to liberation.

Transformation Body — See Three Bodies.

Twelve Links of Cause and Effect

(1) Ignorance ⟷ (2) action ⟷ (3) consciousness ⟷ (4) name and form ⟷ (5) the six sense organs (i.e.,

eye, ear, nose, tongue, body, and mind) ⟷ (6) contact, touch ⟷ (7) sensation, feeling ⟷ (8) thirst, desire, craving ⟷ (9) laying hold of, grasping ⟷ (10) being, existing ⟷ (11) birth ⟷ (12) old age, death.

Vajra

"Diamond," "Thunderbolt," or "Indestructible." 1) The scepter of spiritual nobility and power, used by Tantrikas, which represents yogic technique. Complementary to the ghanta. 2) Indestructible truth in either the functional aspect of purifying all suffering and destroying all mental distortions, or the absolute aspect of Buddha-nature which is primordial, pristine awareness. This is described as being immovable, indivisible, imperishable, and all-encompassing.

Vajrayana

"Diamond Vehicle." The essence of the Buddha's realization as expressed in direct transformation of human potentials and awareness. It is also another name for Tantrayana, a form of Buddhism utilizing a series of books and methods concerned with special yogic practices for swiftly attaining Buddhahood; the third and final interpretation of the Buddha's teachings.

How to Take Refuge in Grand Master Lu

There are three ways of taking refuge in Master Lu and becoming a disciple of the True Buddha Lineage:

1. In person
Make an appointment ahead of time to visit the "True Buddha Tantric Quarter" in Redmond, Washington, USA to receive direct initiation empowerment from Master Lu.

2. By writing
It is often not possible for someone who lives far away to come in person to take refuge. Those students who desire to take refuge can, on the first or fifteenth of any lunar month, at 7:00 a.m., while facing the direction of the rising sun, recite three times the Fourfold Refuge Mantra: "Namo guru bei, namo buddha ye, namo dharma ye, namo sangha ye" and prostrate three times.

On the first or fifteenth of every lunar month, at True Buddha Tantric Quarter, Master Lu performs a ceremony of "remote initiation empowerment" — to give empowerment to all the students who could not journey in person.

A student who takes refuge from a distance, after performing the rites at home, only needs to send a letter to the True Buddha Tantric Quarter stating that he/she is seeking refuge, together with his/her name, address, age, and a small fee for making offerings to the Buddhas. Upon receiving the letter, Master Lu will send a certificate, a picture of the master, and a note stating the level of practice he/she should start with. The address of the True Buddha Tantric Quarter is:

> Sheng-yen Lu
> 17102 NE 40th Ct.
> Redmond, WA 98052, USA
> Tel:(206)882-0916

3. Through local chapters of the True Buddha School
Contact nearby local chapters of the True Buddha School. In San Francisco Bay Area, contact the Purple Lotus Society, 636 San Mateo Ave San Bruno, CA 94066, USA Tel: (415) 952-9513, Fax: (415) 952-9567.

The Purple Lotus Society holds regular group meditation practice every Saturday at 8:00p.m.(open to public, free). Everybody is welcome.

Local Chapters of the True Buddha School in Northern America

Ling Shen Ching Tze Temple
17012 NE 40th Ct.
Redmond, WA 98052
T:(206)882-0916

True Buddha Diamond Temple
29 Forsyth St. 3 FL
New York, NY 10002-6001
T:(212)274-1846, F:(718)417-5192

Chicago Truth Buddhist Society
515 W. Ogden Ave
Downers Grove, IL 60515
T:(708)241-9511, F:(708)717-8209

Chicago North Buddhist Society
5069 N. Broadway
Chicago, IL 60640
T:

Purple Lotus Society
636 San Mateo Ave
San Bruno, CA 94066
T:(415)952-9513, F:(415)952-9567

Rey Tseng Buddhist Association
13020 Ramona Blvd
Baldwin Park, CA 91706
T:(310)327-4847, F:(310)327-4913

Ming Chi Tang
1758 Orchard Hill Lane
Hacienda Heights, CA 91745
T:(818)912-9107

Mui Yin Tong
131 Ladera St
Monterey Park, CA 91754
T:(818)289-4732, F:(818)281-5032

Zen-Insight Society
1601 E. 4th St
Charlotte, NC 28211, USA
H:704-364-3104,O:704-366-3156

Hui Yuen Tang
12810 Mission Circle
Anchorage, AK 99516, USA
T:(907)345-4401, F:(907)248-6738

Houston True Buddha Chapter
10900 Roark Rd.
Houston, TX 77099
T:(713)495-6565

Guam True Buddha Chapter
P.O. Box 3146
Agana, Guam 96910, USA
Tel:(671)789-1079,(617)477-9374

Kwan Chao Tang
1612 Frontage Rd
Cherry Hill, NJ 08034
T:(609)795-3055

Chin Yin Tang Buddhist Society
10853-98 St.
Edmonton, Alberta
Canada T5H 2P6
T:(403)423-0447, F:(403)457-9822

PTT Buddhist Society
514 Keefer St.
Vancouver, B.C.
Canada V6A 1Y3
T:(604)255-3811, F:(604)255-8894

Chan Hai Lei Zang
C.P. 609 Succ. Desjardins
Montreal PQ
Canada H5B 1B7
T:(514)875-9578, F:(514)733-3352

Jing Sim Branch
21 Milliken Blvd., Unit C3
Scarborough, Ont.
Canada M1V 1V3
Tel:416-298-1069,403-474-0986

Pai Yuin Tang
117-28th Ave, N.E.
Calgary, Alberta
Canada
T:(403)250-9282, F:(403)250-7840

Pure Moon Buddhist Association
2517 Danforth Ave
Toronto, Ont.
Canada M4C 1L2
T:(416)690-7803, F:(416)733-7780

Books available from Amitabha Publishing:

Inner World of the Lake
by Master Sheng-yen Lu

In this book, Master Lu weaves the insights he has at the edge of the Lake Sammamish (in Washington State) with his episodes of seeing Dakinis above the Lakes, saving water spirits, and reading messages on the mirror of the Lake. The Lake is no longer an ordinary body of water in Master Lu's sight but is transformed into the Lake of Self Nature (Buddha Nature). Sharing his thoughts, feelings, and happenings at the edge of the Lake, in simple but graceful language, the reader can easily glimpse into the mind of this enlightened sage, and comprehend the esoteric wisdom of Tantric Buddhism. The appendices provides valuable teachings on some of the basics of Tantric Buddhist Practices.

220 pages $13.95 retail

Four Essays on Karma
by Lui Fan Yuen

Written back in the Ming Dynasty, this book contains many gems on how to transform one's karma. The workings of the laws of cause and effect come to life in the many examples outlined in the book. The book follows the lives of various individuals faced with difficult circumstances and how they were able to avert them and live a successful life by understanding the concept of karma. What is more the techniques mentioned in the book for transmuting karma are simple and easy to apply by anyone at anytime to achieve a better life.

Available 11/93

For an up-to-date catalog, write:
Amitabha Publishing
P.O. Box 282188
San Francisco, CA 94128-2188

蓮生活佛盧勝彥金剛根本上師著作年表(1)
Bibliography of Grand Master Sheng-yen Lu (1)

1. A Wisp of Smoke 《淡煙集(新詩), 1967.8》
2. Brief Exchanges in the Garden of Dreams 《夢園小語, 1967.9》
3. Scattering Dreams of Blue 《飛散藍夢, 1968.2》
4. A Leaf Flying in the Wind 《風中葉飛, 1968.11》
5. The Ever-Burning Lamp 《無盡燈(風的聯想), 1972.10》
6. Reflections from Deep Contemplation 《沈思的語花, 1973.5》
7. Blunt Blade of My Thought 《我思的斷片, 1973.8》
8. Manifesting Abundance 《財源滾滾術, 1973.8》
9. Letters to Li 《給麗小札, 1973.12》
10. The Peculiar Phenomena of the Business World
    《企業怪相, 1974.2》
11. Voices From a Pilgrim's Heart 《旅人的心聲, 1974.5》
12. Short Essays on Frustration 《悵惘小品, 1974.10》
13. Within the Mind's Window 《心窗下(夢園小語[二]), 1974.11》
14. Quotations of Successful People 《成功者箴言(正), 1975.2》
15. More Quotations of Successful People
    《成功者箴言(續), 1975.2》
16. Experiences in Spiritual Reading 《靈機神算漫談, 1975.4》
17. A Little Talk by the Southside Window 《南窗小語, 1975.6》
18. Beyond the Green Mountains 《青山之外, 1975.8》
19. My Communications with the Spirit World
    《靈與我之間, 1975.8》
20. More Experiences in Spiritual Reading
    《靈機神算漫談(續), 1975.11》
21. Reaching Higher Spiritual Dimensions 《靈魂的超覺, 1976春》
22. How to Awaken One's Spirit 《啓靈學, 1976春》
23. Case Studies on Earth Magic 《神秘的地靈, 1976夏》
24. Spiritual Confessions 《靈的自白書, 1976.5》
25. More Spiritual Confessions 《靈的自白書(續), 1976.7》
26. Magical Powers 《玄秘的力量, 1976.10》
27. The World of Spirit 《靈的世界, 1977.1》
28. Personal Reflections by a Tranquil Spring
    《泉聲幽記, 1977.3》
29. Earth Magic: Case Studies and Principles
    《地靈探勝玄理, 1977.5》
30. Zen Sky Hut: Collected Writings 《禪天廬什記, 1977.7》
31. The Flying Carpet of The East 《東方的飛氈, 1977.9》

蓮生活佛盧勝彥金剛根本上師著作年表(2)
Bibliography of Grand Master Sheng-yen Lu (2)

32. A Small Vessel of Contemplations 《載著靈思的小舟, 1978.1》
33. The Amazing Power of Karma 《命運的驚奇, 1978.3》
34. The Secrets of Reincarnation 《輪迴的秘密, 1978.7》
35. The Temperament of a Clay Saint 《泥菩薩的火氣, 1978.11》
36. Tales and Mysteries 《傳奇與異聞, 1979.3》
37. The Gift of Revealed Guidance 《神奇的錦囊, 1980.4》
38. Sheng-Yen Lu: On the Realm of Spirit 《盧勝彥談靈, 1981.2》
39. The True Word of the High Spirit 《異靈的真諦, 1981.11》
40. Secret Taoist Method of Spiritual Communication
    《通靈秘法書, 1982.12》
41. The World as Revealed by Spiritual Sight
    《第三眼世界, 1983.1》
42. The Great Spanning Rainbow of Magical Charms
    《靈仙飛虹法, 1983.2》
43. Earth Magic and Spirit 《地靈仙蹤, 1983.3》
    — The Wisdom of Mountain and River 《副標題: 山川的大智慧》
44. Spiritual Warfare in Cultivation 《伏魔平妖傳, 1983.5》
45. Attaining Realization Through Sitting Meditation
    《坐禪通明法, 1983.6》
46. The Cultivator from Seattle 《西雅圖的行者, 1983.8》
47. The Bon Religion and Sorcery 《黑教黑法, 1983.10》
48. The Realization of The Master 《上師的證悟, 1983.12》
49. The Method of Vajrayana 《靈仙金剛大法, 1984.1》
50. The Fierce Protector's Stance 《金剛怒目集, 1984.4》
51. Highest Yoga Tantra and Mahamudra 《無上密與大手印, 1984.5》
52. A Little Taste of Zen 《小小禪味, 1984.4》
53. Between Buddha and Mara 《佛與魔之間, 1984.8》
    — Writings on Spiritual Imbalance
      《副標題: 走火入魔的大探討》
54. Tantric Magic: A Collection 《密宗羯魔法, 1984.10》
55. A Detailed Exposition of Mahamudra 《大手印指歸, 1984.12》
56. The Teaching of Dzogchen, or The Great Perfection
    《密教大圓滿, 1985》
57. Legends of Taoist Transmission 《道法傳奇錄, 1985.4》
*58. The Mystical Experiences of True Buddha Disciples
    《皈依者的感應, 1985.5》
59. The True Buddha Way 《真佛法語, 1985.7》

蓮生活佛盧勝彥金剛根本上師著作年表(3)
Bibliography of Grand Master Sheng-yen Lu (3)

蓮生活佛盧勝彥金剛根本上師著作年表(4)
Bibliography of Grand Master Sheng-yen Lu (4)

87. The Waterfalls of Sacred Light 《神秘的五彩繽紛, 1990.5》
88. A Walk by the Lotus Pond 《蓮花池畔的信步, 1990.7》
89. Dream Experiences of the Disciples 《真佛夢中夢, 1990.9》
90. The Swallow's Flight 《燕子東南飛, 1990.11》
91. A Million Hands Extended 《千萬雙膜拜的手, 1991.1》
92. Cloud like Experiences in Spiritual Absorption
　　《禪定的雲箋, 1991.2》
93. The Cold Damp of Winter 《西雅圖的冬雨, 1991.4》
94. Magnificent Displays of Spiritual Light Phenomena
　　《殊勝莊嚴的雲集, 1991.6》
95. Golden Words from Grand Master Lu 《盧勝彥的金句, 1991.8》
96. The Essence of My Teaching 《蓮生活佛的心要, 1991.10》
97. Romantic Letters to a Monk 《寫給和尚的情書, 1991.12》
98. Transpersonal Experiences in the Ocean of Beings
　　《法海鉤玄, 1992.2》
99. Evening Rain: Reflections of a Lineage Founder
　　《西城夜雨, 1992.4》
100. The 100th Book: Stages of My Writing Career
　　《第一百本文集, 1992.5》
101. The Colorful Butterflies: A Collection
　　《蝴蝶的風采, 1992.9》
102. Tasting the Nectar of The Teaching 《甘露法味, 1992.11》
103. A Collection of Extraordinary Tantric Transformations
　　《密教大相應, 1993.2》
104. Across the Archipelago 《層層山水秀, 1993.5》
105. A Rainbow Villa Snow Storm 《彩虹山莊飄雪, 1993.6》
106. The Living Lamp of The True Buddha 《真佛的心燈, 1993》
*English translation available from Amitabha Publishing